S. J. Stone

The Knight of Intercession

And other Poems

THE
KNIGHT OF INTERCESSION

AND OTHER POEMS

BY

S. J. STONE, M.A.

PEMBROKE COLLEGE, OXFORD
VICAR OF ST. PAUL'S, HAGGERSTON

Νυνὶ δὲ μένει
πιστις, ἐλπὶς, ἀγάπη,
τὰ τρία ταῦτα.
I. COR. XIII. 13.

Ὅ,ττι καλόν, φίλον ἐστί· τὸ δ' οὐ καλόν, οὐ φίλον ἐστί.
THEOGNIS.

THIRD EDITION

RIVINGTONS

London, Oxford, and Cambridge

1875

To the Church.

These at thy feet are laid, for CHRIST, in CHRIST:
Too little worthy of thy Lord and thee:
Yet often unto love hath love sufficed
For merit of its gift; so may it be.
Thou lovest: for thou art of Him Whose grace
Is not by measure, and doth not despise:
And I—as one who e'en before His Face
And the deep test of those reproachful eyes
Could still plead truly—his own vision dim
Not less by love than fear—' Thou knowest this
Who knowest all'—so now, for HIM, in HIM,
Bold in true love, and sure I shall not miss
A mother's grace, this birthday offering
In hope and memory to thy feet I bring.

ST. MARK'S DAY, 1872.

Preface.

MANY of the following Poems have appeared separately at intervals during the past ten years; but the rest, of which the last written is 'The Sea of Galilee,' have not been hitherto published. The Title of the Book is not intended to be specially distinctive: the 'Knight of Intercession' is only thus put forward because it happens to be the longest of the 'Earlier Poems.'

Two of the twelve Hymns in *Lyra Fidelium* are reprinted among those contained in the last section of this volume. The best known of these, 'The Church's one Foundation,' is included, at the instance of those who wish it to be seen as it stood before it was abridged (with the author's sanction) for the Hymnals.

It may be as well to state that, except in the case of the first section, no chronological order of composition has been observed in the arrangement of the Poems.

The author has only further to say that, with more than one aim in view in the publication of these

Poems, he has none other in chief than this: that they may be permitted to tend in the Church to that joyful service of God, in courage, and with a quiet mind, which should mark the life of the redeemed.

S. J. S.

St. Paul's Vicarage, Haggerston,
April 25, 1872.

Preface to Third Edition.

This Edition differs from the First and Second by the removal of ten of the Poems, and by the addition of twenty-three. Two of the 'Earlier Poems' have been omitted, one of the Miscellaneous Section, and seven of the Hymns.

The additions comprise a new 'Idyll of Deare Childe' on page 77, the Poems on pages 225 and 228, twelve Sonnets from page 279 to 287, and eight Hymns from page 325 to 346.

It only remains for the author to thank both critics and readers for the kindly reception of the volume hitherto.

Sept. 30, 1874.

S. J. Stone

The Knight of Intercession
And other Poems

ISBN/EAN: 9783337294496

Printed in Europe, USA, Canada, Australia, Japan

Cover: Foto ©Thomas Meinert / pixelio.de

More available books at **www.hansebooks.com**

Contents.

Earlier Poems.

	PAGE
The Knight of Intercession, ...	1
Down Stream to London, written in Temple Gardens, London, in memory of March 19-23, 1861, .	11
In Memoriam. E. B. Browning. Obiit MDCCCLXI.,	17
'Sublatum ex Oculis.' A Sonnet, . .	20
Good-bye to Oxford, . .	21

The Idylls of Deare Childe.

I. Deare Childe, . . .	27
II. 'Morning Robert,'	36
III. The Quest of Love. A Parish Idyll, .	53
IV. The Rectory Farm. A Parish Idyll,	77

Poems on Pictures.

Death as a Friend. On the Picture 'Der Tod als Freund,'	101
Tired. On a Picture of a Tired Child, .	109

	PAGE
Saint Augustine and Monica. On the Picture by Ary Scheffer, ...	112
Setting Sail. On a Picture of Three Children on the Shore, ...	118
Christus Consolator. On the Picture by Ary Scheffer, illustrative of the Saviour's invitation, 'Come unto me, all ye that labour and are heavy-laden, and I will give you rest,'	121
The Cradle on the Shore. On the Picture by Eugene West, ...	132
A Boy's Reverie over an old Picture, . . .	134
The Soliloquy of a Rationalistic Chicken. On the Picture of a newly-hatched Chicken contemplating the Fragments of its native Shell, . . .	137
Country-Born. On a Picture of a Farm-yard, .	140
A Sea-side Reverie, ...	142

Miscellaneous Poems.

The Sea of Galilee, .	149
The Gate of Death,	165
The Birdie, ...	173
What the Mountain said to the Maiden, .	182
The Maiden's Reply to the Mountain,	186
Trust, ...	192
Lententide. A Meditation,	196
Coming Holy Week,	200
Easter Eve,	202

	PAGE
The Bird of Grace,	207
The Answer of the Hills,	213
The Meditation of Isaac,	219
The Bishop of Winchester. In Memoriam,	225
A Sick-Bed Confirmation,	228

Songs.

The Beautiful Death. (Song of a Cavalier's Mother),	235
Christ's Knight,	237
The Ebb of Tide,	238
The Sea's Amen,	241
Children's Song by the Sea,	243
The Harvest of Souls,	245
Lullaby of Life,	247

Sonnets.

The One Name,	251
Trust,	252
Good Friday,	253
The Same,	254
Easter Sonnets—	
I. Mary Magdalene on Easter Morning,	255
II. The Gardener,	256
III. The Greeting,	257
The Salutation of the Elders,	258
The Same,	259
The Small-pox in the East—	
I. The Sisters of Mercy,	260

		PAGE
II. Church Ministrations,	.	261
III. A Private Baptism, .	.	262
IV. Death and Life, ...	.	263
V. The Things seen and the Things not seen,	.	264
VI. Spring and Easter, . . .	.	265
VII. Holy Communion, ...	.	266
A Sunday Confirmation in an East-End Church,	.	267
The Same, ...	.	268
A Morning Present of Spring Flowers, . .	.	269
The Same, ...	.	270
John Addington Symonds, M.D. Ceased to practise 1869, Died February 25, 1871, . . .	.	271
The Same, ...	.	272
Windsor Parish Church Reconstructed, . .	.	273
In Charterhouse Chapel: on Founder's Day, 1872,	.	274
The Same, ...	.	275
To Windsor Cemetery on May-day		
I. Through the Park, ...	.	276
II. The Cemetery, . . .	.	277
III. The Little Church, . . .	.	278
Lord Derby. 'Sans Changer,'		279
Bishop Gray. In Memoriam, . . .	.	280
Evensong in Lichfield Cathedral, on the Feast of Epiphany, Jan. 6, 1873, . . .		283
Midnight in London (February 24, 1873), .	.	286
Worcester Cathedral (Reopened Wednesday, April 8, 1874, ...	.	287

Hymns.

	PAGE
'I believe in the Holy Catholic Church, the Communion of Saints,'	293
'I believe in the Forgiveness of Sins,'	296
Battle Hymn for the New Year,	298
The River of God,	300
Light at Eventide,	303
The Attraction of the Cross,	305
The Perfect Day,	307
Holy Communion,	309
The Travail of the Creation,	311
The Prisoners of Hope,	313
The Glorious Three,	315
The 'Athletes of the Universe,'	317
The Church's Song,	319
Hymn of Thanksgiving for the Recovery of H.R.H. The Prince of Wales,	321
The Transfiguration,	325
Hymns for the Day of Intercession—	
I. For Colonial Missions,	328
II. For Missions to the Heathen,	331
III. Hymn of Thanksgiving,	334
Saint Mark, Evangelist and Martyr,	337
Hymn of Church Defence,	340
Confirmation Litany Hymn,'	343
'In Thee.' A Hymn for Church Workers,	346

Earlier Poems.

1859-1862.

The Knight of Intercession.

> 'All things pass away but the Love of God. Suffice it then to say that he loved and feared God above all things.'—*From 'The Character of Bayard,' by his 'Loyal Serviteur.'*

IN ancient days, so saith an old Romaunt,[1]
   There lived a knight, brave, rich, and nobly born,
Withal pure-hearted as a saint, whose love
His ladye spurned; not that she loved him not,
Although she said so, but because she saw
He put God higher than all human claims
Of love and reverence. So she bade him go,
And spurned him for a wicked pride: and he,
Not caring any more to dwell with men
In open converse, left his ancient halls
And things of wealth and state, which men hold dear,
And rode through many lands for many a day,
Doing true devoir as a noble knight.

[1] This legend, though here materially altered in detail and significance, owes its origin in outline to a story by Captain Whyte Melville, first published in *Fraser's Magazine*.

None knew him, for he lived with visor down;
His harness of plain steel revealed no sign
Of rank or name; nor bore he in his helm
Token or favour; only on his shield
A dark cross, as of mourning. On he rode;
And ever as he wrought a gallant deed,
And man or maiden asked him, 'How may I
Repay thy service?' never aught said he
Save, 'Pray for Her!' and parted, still in quest
Of fresh occasion, and for guerdon still
Took nothing; only came the self-same voice
From the closed helm in answer: 'Pray for Her!'

And so the captive freed did pray for Her;
The rescued maiden prayed; the widow prayed,
With all her wrongs avenged; the poor and rich,
Each for the service they received from him,
Did pray for Her. The little children lost
In the wild wood, and found by him, and saved
From wolf or robber, lifting trustful eyes
Prayed also: and the angels went and came,
Bearing those prayers, and bringing blessings down.
And so she prospered much in all her pride.

The days passed on; and on the warrior rode—
The Knight of Intercession: and his deeds

Made the plain harness famous in the lands;
And neither ceased those grateful hearts to pray,
Nor she to prosper.   Came a day at last,
Whereon a certain prince, with all his host,
Did battle for his kingdom; and the foe
Had well-nigh driven back his last essay,
And won the city. Mothers, sisters, wives,
Wringing their frantic hands upon the towers,
Wept for the coming issue, death or shame.
Then on a sudden rode into the fray
The nameless knight: the foremost foe drew back
Before his onset; then with terrible blows
He clave a bloody pathway to their chief,
And bore him down, and slew him, and pressed on
To win the standard. So the battle changed;
The prince and all his warriors took fresh heart,
And drove their foemen backward toward the sea,
And overthrew them. When the fight was done,
The prince with all his nobles came to thank
The saviour of his kingdom. But he lay
Wounded upon the standard he had won;
A lance was in his breast, and through the helm
He was sore smitten: and at last was seen

Through the raised visor the long-hidden face,
Sad, pale, and noble. Then the prince burst forth:
'Sir Knight, what guerdon wilt thou for thine aid?
Certes, whatever thou shalt ask is thine,
E'en to the one half of my realm!' And so
The nobles prayed him; and their ladies came
And wept their thanks; and all in that great town—
The rich and poor, the old and young—came there,
Beseeching him with tears of joy, that he
Would name some guerdon. And the knight looked
    round;
O'er his pale visage moved a moment's smile—
Like the last tinge of sunset on a height—
Tender and holy, moving men to tears;
And smiling thus, he murmured, 'Pray for Her!'
Then with closed eyes he lay a little space,
And the pale face grew paler, and his head
Grew heavier on the knees of him whose hands
Had caught him falling. Yet once more the eyes
Were opened, and the noble head was raised,
And once more, while his upward wistful gaze
Sought the far heav'n, he murmured, 'Pray for Her!'
And in the look and in the prayer he died.

    And in that kingdom never passed a day,

But prince, knights, nobles, ladies, young and old,
And rich and poor, at morn and evensong,
Did evermore henceforward pray for Her.

Ere long there came unto the ladye's bower
A nameless messenger. 'I come,' said he,
'Ladye, I come from one who loved thee well,
And whom thou lovest!' Then the ladye flushed,
And but he said 'who *loved*,' and not 'who *loves*,'
And so awoke a terror in her breast,
Which still was mindful of the love it spurned,
She would have straight dismissed him. Still she
    feigned,
And dallying with her fear she answered him
Lightly and falsely: 'Comest thou from him,
The stately earl of yonder proud domain,
Who bids me make him and his fair broad lands
Mine own?' He answered sternly, 'Not from him;
His heart is narrow, though his lands are broad!'
'Perchance thou comest from the courtly knight
Who wears my glove for crest, my woven scarf
Across his gilded harness?' 'Not from him;
His sword is rusty, though he rides in gold!'
'Thou comest then, I wot, from him who rules

In yonder city, treads his palace floors,
And sighs for me?' He answered, 'Not from him;
His name is noble, but his soul is mean!'

So thrice she questioned, hovering round her fear,
As one who stays and lingers at a door
Wistful, yet dreads to enter. So she paused:
Then with changed voice demanded, 'Comest thou—?'
But here she sickened, for she felt his eyes
Looked sadly on her, seeing through her soul,
Right to the inner trouble, undeceived
By outward seeming. Then she summoned strength,
And asked in accents tremulous and low,
Which grew in force and passion—as a stone,
Loosed from a hill-side, rolls towards the vale,
Slowly at first, but gathering power and speed
Falls wildly—'Comest thou from him, my knight,
Nameless but famous, unknown but renowned,
In plain steel armour, with his visor down,
Yet winning noblest praise in all the lands;
Who knew not that I loved him even then
When I was scornfullest, whom yet I love,
Whom I love on for ever? If from him
Thou comest, get thee back and tell him all!
Go tell him I repent me of my pride;

Tell him I wait for him, and spend my heart
In waiting; tell him that I never loved
And never shall love other till I die!
Speak! comest thou from him?'
        He said, 'From him.'
And more the trembling passion of her frame,
The close-clasped hands, the cheek now red, now pale,
And more the pleading hunger of her eyes,
Than her quick asking, moved him to reply
Softly, and not in wrath, 'I come from him,
Ladye—from him who cannot come to thee;
For now that visor closed is closed no more,
For men have looked beneath it; and he sleeps
In that plain harness, never more to rise
Till God shall wake him. In a prayer he died,
That all he saved and served should pray for thee.
So until death, at morn and evensong,
True hearts and hands are lifted up for thee,
That all things of the earth, and all of heaven,
In all thy goings out and comings in,
May bless thee always, even to the end.
Farewell! so pray a thousand hearts for thee;
So shall I pray for ever unto death:
Farewell!'

    She heard him speechless to the close,
And speechless still she saw him pass away :
'Death,' and 'Farewell,' the last words on his lips,
And in her ears. Oh, how they rose and fell
Alternate, like a cadence of despair !
Death and Farewell ! Farewell and Death ! in each
A hopeless issue, speaking not of him
Who said them, but of him from whom he came—
Her own true knight, her noble, peerless knight :
Death and Farewell ! and then it seemed to her
As though she too must die.
       Her maidens came
And found her swooning.
         But she did not die :
She woke again to hate the thought of life,
Yet fearing death. She stood as one might stand,
A pilgrim for whose steps is no return,
With choice for two ways : one across a wild
Gloomy and drear, the other through a vale
With unknown terrors lurking in its depths,
More drear because unknown. E'en so she looked
On life and death : the one a darkened path,
Reft of the sun which might have shone on her ;
So darkened now, that ever and anon

Stretching her hopeless hands out in the dark
Towards that other, 'Oh, that I might die!'
She cried—still conscious that she dared not die.

  Then was it well for her that late and soon,
From great and noble, from the small and mean—
The sad and needy, and the rich and glad—
From little children and hoar-headed men—
The voice of intercession ever rose,
Like incense, unto Him 'Who heareth prayer.'
For even while He smote her with a sense
Of hopelessness and anguish—even then
He wrought within her unto final good.
Crushing her pride, He bade her stoop and raise
That Cross she had refused of lowly fear,
And love unselfish.
                Then He gave her peace—
Because her heart had learned to rest on Him—
His perfect peace: and with rejoicing flight,
The great good angels of a thousand prayers—
The prayers still rising morn and eve for her—
Sped downwards at commandment of their King,
And tended her with constant service; filled
Her mind with holy thoughts and pure desires
And glorious hopes. And so it was that she,

Who looked on life and death with hate and fear,
Saw in her life a happy pilgrimage
On toward a better country, which she sought
With longing; and in death that blessed stream,
Ordained to bear the children of the Lord
Beyond the shadowy twilight of this world,
Into the glory of the perfect day.

Down Stream to London.

Written in Temple Gardens, London, in memory of March 19-23, 1861.

THE din of the great town is on my ears
    And not the voices of the wood and wave,
And the lark's warbling: the pure air and sky,
With its cloud isles and mountains, is all past;
Above me stretches the thick smoke and mist
That shuts heaven from the city; and no more
Beneath me glides the king of silver streams,
The river of all rivers—yon black flood
That surges past me now and bears its name
Is not the Thames I know, the Thames I love.

Oh for the gleaming river once again,
That seemed to bear us through a golden age
In those four days: woods, meadows, hamlets, farms,
Spires in the vale, and towers upon the hill,
The great chalk quarries glaring thro' the shade,
The pleasant lanes and hedgerows, and those homes
Which seemed the very dwellings of content
And peace and sunshine—oh for the fresh lawns

That ran down brightly to the water's edge
To drink the waves—with freshness never known
In all the glow and glare of other lands.
Oh for the music of the livelong day,
The songs of woods and waters, and the lark
Cleaving his way through the thin air to heaven,
With that loud carol like a spirit freed
From chains and darkness.   How we sometimes paused
And let the boat glide at the river's will,
And how, in the short pause, upon our ears,
Far in the distance downwards, there would come
A murmur from the cataract that flowed
Off from the side-stream—first a low deep hum,
A very dream of waters; louder then,
And still more loud as the swift boat sped on
Nearer and nearer; now the full-toned flood
Drowns with majestic thunder voice and oar
Till the boat bears us past it; and the sound
Throws after us its harmony, and then
Subsides again into the dream and dies.

   The spirit of the Spring was in the woods,
And woke within them murmurs that expressed

A joy of expectation, very low,
A musing gladness like the voice of one
Who whispers doubts because he is so sure:
A prelude to the burst of happy song
That hails fruition of the promised joy,
The march of coming Summer through the land.

Never without our music! When the woods,
Left far behind, were lost to ear and eye,
Or yet below unreached for sight and sound;
When trees were rare, or seen far off unheard
Along the level; when the waterfalls—
Melodious visitations far between—
Were no more with us; when the lark was down
Among the furrows, and the rise and fall
Of that aërial fountain of sweet sound
Was silent for a season—then perchance
Would float the chime of bells upon the breeze
From some old tower, or sound of happy life
From some bright village, or with distant hum,
And deepening roll, and palpitating roar,
Charged down the great fire chariot of the train,
And passed us like a whirlwind and went by.
Nor seldom too the boat and we sped on

With silence on the banks and on the stream
Save the long swish of oars, the dip, the stroke
That hurled the troubled water far astern
In little battling whirlpools, soon at peace;
And that was real music in our ears.
As men that wander upon alien shores
Hear some loved song of their own land again,
And feel their blood run quicker: so that sound
Kept ever stirring pleasant memories
Of many a bright laborious afternoon
On the old Isis; grim experiences
Of training pulls in eight oars—down the course
To Iffley, past the lasher, through the lock,
Then on to Sandford, turn, and home again
From Iffley racing-pace—'lift, lift,' and in
From Saunders' bridge 'at 40!' Oh the grind
We grumbled at, and loved so for its worth,
So far above all else for growth of strength
And moral muscle: then those mighty days
That brought the Races; oh the toil, the strife—
Upon the stream, the rushing regular oars,
'The music of the many as of one,'
The forward shoot of straightened backs and arms,
Then the strong lift together; on the shore

A shouting frantic crowd—a victory here,
There a defeat as glorious!—those were days
Which memory fostered in her safest hold
And needed little spur to wake again.
  So passed the time—a time that fled on wings
Too eager for our liking: and at last
We lost the green fields and the pleasant woods,
With all their happy voices and glad scenes
Of beauty and repose. The stream grew dark,
The light shone fainter through a sky less clear,
The approaching city tainted wave and air.
But still we failed not of a fitting close
To such a voyage. Came a day, our last,
Which saw us waiting, watching on the shore,
Among ten thousand eager too as we
To see the issue—which should bear the palm,
Our Isis or the Cam, for stalwart sons,
Broad backs and chests and iron-sinewed arms
Knit with a resolute courage and strong will
That shunned not stormy weeks of toil and pains
To weld their strength with hard-learnt skill, and win
The mastery of the waters—aye, and prove
In whose veins flowed the truest purest stream
Of Viking blood and spirit. On they came—

The throbbing expectation where we stood,
Far up the course turned every straining eye
To see who led the way—The dark blue oars!
'Tis Oxford wins!—and Cambridge far behind
Rallied in vain, and the great race was won.
Be no more said, but that the victor's fame,
Which pales not set beside the brightest years,
Sheds lustre on the vanquished, with a grace
For such a fruitless struggle. But for us
More than for others 'twas a day indeed
To be remembered, crowning such a time
With such a sequel. Now it is all past,
And all that bright experience of the Thames
Is but a memory:—but although my eyes,
In this broad water flowing darkly past,
See little to recall the clear bright flood
That bore us down so blithely those four days,
Yet still it bears thy name, and even here,
Thou true Pactolus! heart and voice are fain,
Despite thy smoky shores and clouded waves,
To give thee all their little, and heap up
Full phrase and epithet to speak my love
And swell thy praise- thou paragon of streams,
Thou lovely, lordly, mild, majestic Thames!

In Memoriam.—E. B. Browning.

OBIIT MDCCCLXI.

NOT, Florence, for the glory of thy skies,
   For those grand mountains, for the golden flow
Of sweet-voiced Arno through the vale below,
Not for the Eden land that round thee lies
With claim for fairest in a land most fair,
Do men award thee such a crown to wear

Among the nations. In thee lived and loved
That Dante whom men call 'The Florentine'
(And spite thine old contempt his fame is thine);
In thee Savonarola died and proved
His indignation righteous; and in thee
Giotto built an immortality:

These names, nor these alone, do give thy name
A greater glory e'en than Nature's hand
In all her large grace to thy Tuscan land,
Seen through the dark of ages like a flame:

And now, behold, another Memory throws
A fair fresh leaf upon thy crownèd brows.

Now doubly is our English homage won,
That thou hast nursed with such a tender care
An English flower too frail for English air,
With thy sweet breezes, and thy radiant sun:
And doubly art thou dear that in thee lies
All of our greatest poetess that dies.

Ah! songless now the full-toned utterance
That spake the language of such lofty thought
And passionate feeling to such music wrought,
What time from Casa Guidi o'er th' expanse
Of men and minds she gazed on Italy,
Vexed and upheaving like a troubled sea.

Lost is the singer that so nobly sang
God's Truth and Beauty:—closed the wondrous eyes
That saw so much of heaven beneath the skies:
Silent the clarion that so sweetly rang:
And passed the poet from us to that throng
Where all are poets of diviner song.

The 'Wine of Cyprus' flows for her no more
Who drinks of better fountains: mysteries,
Of which she sang in vision, now she sees
Revealed behind the veil on the far shore,
In the clear light of that eternal day
Which after dawning fadeth not away.

The 'Drama of *her* Exile' is all done,
And now with earthly mists no longer dim
Her eyes are rapt upon those 'Seraphim'
To see whose 'wondrous faces' round the throne,
And hear whose 'most sweet music,' in past lay
Our hearts grew solemn as we heard her pray.

And we who read, 'No more vain words be said;'
Seem too to hear the 'near Hosannas' roll;
And in the bliss that crowns the living soul
Forget the sorrow brooding o'er the dead:
Exultant, that the spiritual breath
Triumphs for ever over pain and death.

'Sublatum ex Oculis.'

A SONNET.

'O selfless man and stainless gentleman!'

CHRISTMAS, 1861.

EVEN so, 'God giveth His beloved sleep!'
    And grief o'erwhelms us on this holy morn,
And grief will wait and see the New Year born.
What can we else but bow our heads and weep?
The fountains of our love, new-found, are deep.
For one who lived—and lived in spite of scorn—
A selfless life of use, 'tis meet *we* mourn:
Since having sown he goes elsewhere to reap.
O True and Pure and Royal! round thy brow
We, the once blind, now seeing, sadly weave
Garlands of praise for duty nobly done:
'Great Prince, and man of men,' we know thee now
Too late, save that revering we believe
Thy works shall follow though thy rest is won.

Good-bye to Oxford.

*'Eheu ! fugaces, Postume, Postume,
Labuntur anni.'*

GOOD-BYE at last to Oxford ! with full eyes
 I watch the autumn day grow dark and die,
And see the year put on its saddest guise,
  To sadden this Good-bye.

This sorrowing rain seems but the tearful grief
 That pride forbids although the heart be fain,
And that regretful wind seems the relief,
  In utterance, of pain.

Dim, as I thread the twilight, on my gaze
 The 'glorious street' lies wrapt in misty gloom,
And in grieved sort like statues of past days
  The old towers darkly loom.

I hear 'Old Tom' announce the dying light,
 The deep hoarse voice that I shall hear no more ;
Hoarser and deeper seems the note this night
  Than in the days of yore.

GOOD-BYE TO OXFORD.

Good-bye to walls and towers I know so well,
    And love as dearly—most of all to thine[1]
Wherein my lot 'in pleasant places' fell,
    Kind Nurse and Mother mine!

May Heaven thee prosper! and good-bye to thee,
    My noble Isis, loved so all these years;
Echoes of gallant strife right gloriously
    E'en now ring in mine ears:

And mingling with them comes a measured strain,
    The tramp and music of a marching band;
I fight my bloodless 'battles o'er again,'
    In arms for father-land.

'These 'twill be joy to recollect,' 'tis said,
    Though with a tinge of sorrow, being gone;
Oxford, with me the dead past is not dead,
    Though I must needs pass on.

Should I not love thee? and for more than these,
    By feasts (ah, sought too waywardly!) of thine,
Where sat the Stagyrite, and Socrates,
    And 'Poets poured us wine.'

[1] Pembroke College.

Aye, and for more! by all the eager search
  The wisdom-quest of vague perplexèd youth:
By the One Word made sure; by the One Church
  Known as the Ground of Truth.

Good-bye is 'God be with thee!' Even so
  May God thee keep—above all fears I pray—
Truth's changeless champion, Error's strongest foe,
  Till His own day.

The Idylls of Deare Childe.

I.

Deare Childe.

A PARISH IDYLL.

'Who is the greatest in the Kingdom of Heaven?'

A SIMPLE cross, let in the outer wall
    Under the chancel window, and beneath
A little slab, of marble also, graved
With these two words, spelt anciently, DEARE CHILDE.
These and no more, and yet he lingered here;
He who had wandered with me, and had scanned,
With heedless eyes that cared to rest on none,
The carven annals on a score of tombs.
He who had laughed at this, and sneered at that,
Nor gave elsewhere a reverent word for one,
Yet lingered here, and lingered on, until
I moved away to test him; still he stayed
And kept his eyes upon the simple cross
And those two words; and when I spoke to him

He moved not. Coming back and touching him,
I said, 'What keeps you?' As he turned, I saw
The face was wholly changed, the open brow
Thrid as with pain or thought, the careless eyes
Filmed with a mist of tears, and the strong lips
Set closer, as prepared against a sense
Of quivering weakness. Facing round again
Upon the little monument, he said,
'Tell me of him, or her.' I thereupon,
In sudden memory of a bygone day
And a great loss which dimmed his life awhile,
Knew why the simple words on one unknown
Had power to move him by the touch of that
Which, says the great Bard, 'makes the whole world
    kin.'
So without word of wonder I replied:
'Of her, who underneath the Holy Sign
Sleeps there, the record is but that of all
Who die ere yet the pure baptismal robe
Is soiled, or stained, or torn in this bad world.
Yet there are words of hers I know and keep,
Said in her last hours, little childish words,
Yet all divine in their simplicity,
Pure gold, with no touch of the base alloy

That mars all earthly treasure ; you shall hear,
I am no miser though it is pure gold ;
Share it, it shall enrich your soul as mine.
She was the daughter of a shepherd here,
And born hard by, there, where you see the smoke
Rise from the cottage underneath the eaves
Of that grove-covered hill. He who begot
And she who bare her were and are to me,
Of all the flock on whom I tend for God,
Worthiest of love and honour : poor in truth,
Save in that wealth which passeth not away ;
Humble, save in that greatness which alone
Is lord of death ; not known within the world,
But written amid God's chosen saints ; and she,
This quiet sleeper, was their only child.
Seven years, that fled like Eden hours, was she
The sunshine and the music of their home.
Such blessed sunshine ! in the holy blue
Of innocent eyes, in the fair, guileless face,
And myriad glimmers of her golden hair :
Such music ! in the run of little feet
That beat the merry pulse of laughing hours,
And in the loving prattle of the lips
That framed the simple tale of daily needs,

Of daily hopes and pleasures, aims and ends,
So sweetly, or that spake on holy themes
With all the intuition marvellous,
The fearless, reverent confidence of those
Whose angels see the Father's face in Heaven.
Ah me! perchance that sunshine was too bright
For this all-darkening world, too sweet perchance
That music for the jarring dissonance
Of sin and sorrow. He who loved her best
Did what was best, and we that wept His will
Yet praise Him; praise Him for the treasure lent,
For that sweet angel-visit which unawares
We entertained; for that dear memory
Which makes the past of those seven wingèd years
An Eden of remembrance; more than all
We now have learned to praise Him that again
Into His blessed keeping, undefiled,
He took her back, to meet us at "that day."
You wonder at my speech of "us" and "we,"
As though she had two fathers. She had two—
Him the true, faithful man of whom I spake,
The shepherd of the flocks on yonder wold,
And me, the pastor of the sheep of God
Folded within this vale and on those hills;

His child according to the flesh, and mine
According to the Spirit—mine the arms
In which she died to sin and lived to God;
Mine the priest's hand that traced upon her brow
The token of her new inheritance,
Yon sacred sign; mine, too, the lips that sware
Her vows of fealty. And from that hour,
As by an instinct, I, who had no child,
Gave all the father's heart within my breast
To her, and she to me a daughter's love;
Such love as to the others of her home,
And reverence withal as unto one
Nearest, she held it, unto God and Heaven,
Which coming all so full from one so pure,
Not seldom smote and pricked a heart that knew
Its own defilement.
    So it was, that when
God's message came that we must render up
The treasure lent awhile, to me they gave—
In the wild grief that shook them more than mine,
Marking the severance of the fleshly bond—
The task to tell her that the end was nigh.
I went alone into the little room,
And using the familiar name she knew,

"Dear child," I said, "God wants you very soon
To go to Him. He has a better home
Above, you know, with angels in His Heaven,
Where there is perfect peace and no more pain."
"Oh, that is good," she answered, "no more pain!
It hurts me so, and mother cries to see it;
But, sir, will she come there, and father too,
And you?"

I answered, "But a little while
And we will come; God has not sent for us,
He calls you first, soon He will send for us,
And we will come, and you will meet us there,
And we shall never part, nor grieve, nor die."

"Am I to die, sir?" tremulously she said;
And when I could not speak for sudden tears,
Went on, "Oh, now I know I am to die,
Like little Alice at the farm last year,
Who used to gather flowers and play with me;
But she fell ill, and angels came from God
And took her up, you said, beyond the stars.
But oh! they cried so when she went away!
Will mother cry, and father if I go,
And you, sir? Oh, 'tis sad for you to cry!
May I not stay awhile?"

                    I answered her,
"Your father, mother, and I love you, dear;
You know it!"
                    "Oh, I love you so!" she said.
"But there is One who loves you more than all:
Who loves you best?" I asked her. Then a smile
Childlike and holy, as I never saw
On other lips, so human and divine,
Flowed over all the tender little face,
And broke in utterance, "JESUS loves me best,
JESUS, Who died upon the cross for me!"
   And much it moved me, watching her, to see
How the sweet head before the Holy Name,
Despite the languor of its feebleness,
Essayed the wonted reverence where it lay.
"'Tis JESUS," I replied, "Who loves you best,
That calls you. Will you wait awhile, or go
Now when He calls you?"
                    "Now, oh now," she said,
And smiled again, and clasped her little hands;
"And I shall see His face, and hear His voice,
And He will come and take me in His arms
And say your words, 'dear child,' and bid me rest,
Making me love Him ever more and more.

                    c

And I shall wait for you, and you will come,
And mother dear, and father when He sends,
And He will make us glad and good for ever."

'That noon—for it was morning when I spoke—
There came upon her bitter throes of pain;
But nought save sudden spasms of the brow,
And the shook lips and quicker breath betrayed
The tribulation of the passing life.
No wailing or complaint to vex our ears,
But ever and anon we heard her say,
In whispers softly, "There is no more pain;"
Or she would murmur, "Jesus loves me best,"
And then again would whisper, "No more pain."

'But when the sun was low at eventide,
The bitter pain had passed, and she lay still,
Too weak for words, but smiling peacefully
With eyes that looked upon us with such love,
Our hearts in battle with the struggling tears
Were nigh to bursting. Then we knelt and prayed,
And as we rose the parting sunlight streamed
With its last glory through the window panes,
And o'er the dying child. She could not speak,
But first at us, and after toward the west,

Looked wistfully. And then the mother said
Divining, "She would have you sing the hymn
You taught her for the sunset every day."

  'And so we sang the hymn of eventide,
"Abide with me;" and while we sang, her soul
Sang with us in that marvellous sweet smile,
That was like music too divine for sound.
We sang and darkness deepened, but that smile
Grew brighter yet, and brighter, till the close,
"In life, in death, O Lord, abide with me!"
Then, with "Amen," was breathed one little sigh,
And song, and smile, and soul fled up to heaven.

  'Deare Childe! I think that we thus are more blest
Than by thy life—we are more near to God:
That holy sleep in JESUS which thou sleepest
Has power to lull us also into dreams
More bright of waters still and pastures green,
Where thou art waiting till He bid us come:
He, the Good Shepherd, Who doth feed His flock,
Gather the little lambs within His arm,
And gently lead the heavy laden home.'

II.

'𝔐orning Robert.'

A PARISH IDYLL.

> 'So ere that day and hour begun
> In which Thyself will be the sun;
> Thou'lt find me drest, and on my way,
> Watching the break of Thy Great Day.'
> *The Dawning.*—H. VAUGHAN.

> 'Until the day dawn.'

THERE stands a little cottage near the wood
   That lies one side the village church, and crowns
The long but gentle slope above the vale.
Wide on the left, descending from the wood,
Fringed with a low grey wall of ancient stone,
A grassy park extends, with, here and there,
Great trees, alone or clustered, till it joins
The hamlet and the river.
                   Many years
A pensioner of the Hall, an old man, lived
Alone in the lone cottage. Dear to him

Its narrow walls and weather-beaten thatch,
And windows quaint and dim. There he was born ;
There had his mother loved him ; there she died,
Her hand in his ; there had his father prayed
His latest prayer of blessing on his head ;
There, one fair summer morning, he had brought
From the near church, his pretty sweetheart home ;
There she had loved him well a happy year ;
There, with her little babe, he saw her die.

   Awhile the old dear home seemed changed to him,
Desolate and unlovely, but ere long
The sense of darkness and of loneliness
Left it, for it was peopled from the Past,
And brightened with the Future. There he saw,
As with shut eyes he sat beside his hearth,
The old familiar faces come and go,
And heard their voices at his will ; and there,
Far better thus alone, in simple prayer
And study of the Holy Word, he held
Communion with those dear saints gone before,
Not lost—and in that quiet commune drew
His vision of the glory that should be.

   But when his years were many, and his limbs
Failed at their wonted toil, the good old Squire—

Knowing himself the weight of many years—
Gave him the cottage for his life, and all
The little needs his thrift could not supply,
Supplied with willing hand.

                         But though his limbs
Were feeble, yet his heart had kept its youth,
And something of its childhood: in his eyes
It shone so bright, and over all his face—
Despite the wintry pallor of his age,
And the deep wrinkles which the tide of life,
Receding, had left marked on cheek and brow—
Glowed yet so fresh and cheerly, it belied
His fourscore years. A simple heart it was,
Not learn'd in any lore save that of Heaven;
Yet, in its order, rare, for he was one
Whom God had made a poet to Himself;
Poet, indeed, who 'never wrote a verse,'
Yet none the less a poet. He could hear
Music that did not come to common ears,
And see, what eyes around him seldom saw,
An inner life beneath the outer form
Of Nature: so that, knowing not his gift,
He marvelled that his fellows gave no heed
To that which made his life so sweet to him,

And earth so dear that naught could come amiss.
Spring, Summer, Autumn, Winter, day and night,
The shade and shine, the light of moon and stars,
The clouds of rain, or storm, or rolling mist,
The whirlwind and the zephyr—each and all
Were ministers of pleasure : every one
Taught him of God.
                Those years of solitude
Fed his poetic heart from morn till eve,
From eve till morn ; and each repeated change
Made new delight.
                Often, in simple words,
Glad of an ear that seemed to understand,
He told me how the Months were all his friends,
And had their mission to his heart and soul
With sight or sound; how, not in Spring alone,
Or Summer, was their visitation loved,
But how, not seldom, he would lie awake
Communing on his bed in peace, and hear
The tears of dying Summer dash their drops
Against the thatch, the window, and the door;
While from the drench'd woods came the Autumn
    throes,
Wild shrieks, and hollow moanings of the winds,

That rose with power and died away in pain,
That died in pain and rose again with power,
The long night through. Or in the Winter days,
'I love, sir,' he would say, 'to hear the storm
Go roaring through the glen and down the vale
So strong and terrible; for, as I watch,
It minds me of the Psalm you preached about
A while ago—David on Lebanon,
Hearing the LORD'S voice in the thunder-roll
O'er many waters: how it shook above
The old, eternal mountains, and below
The still, waste land, dividing, as it sped,
The flames of fire; and how the cedar-trees
Brake as it smote them, and the forest depths
Unclosed before it; but, saith he, the LORD
Sitteth above the thunder and the flood,
A King for ever! and will give His own
Strength for the storms of life, and afterward
The blessing of His peace. And so it is
The end is always peace; and therefore, sir,
I love the storm, because the calm at last
Is sure, and sweeter for it.'
       There were none
In all the scattered hamlet did not know

Old Robert; and though there were some to sneer—
Poor souls! they only sneered to hide the shame
Stirred by the pricking judgment in their breasts—
Because his kindly face changed utterly,
Stern, sorrowful, before a godless deed
Or an unholy word; yet he was loved
By most, and honoured; chief of all by those
The furthest from him in the scale of years;
For the child's heart within the aged man
Yearned upon little children, like his Lord's.
No hard disciple he to thrust away
Their clambering feet and clinging hands, or hush
Their eager voices! 'Twas a goodly sight
To see and hear them on a summer day
Around him, like some old-world patriarch
With half a hundred children; or to watch
How in God's house, on every Holy-day,
He, from his wonted station in the aisle,
Beside a grey stone pillar near to them,
Joined, in the holy words of prayer and praise,
His deeper tones with their less tremulous
Sweet voices, and to note how with a look—
The old saint, with the little ones of Christ,
Like some good shepherd whom the young lambs
   know—

He would win back into the ways of prayer
Wandering eyes and hearts.

       An arbiter
In many a village difference was he,
And oracle of counsel in their need
To all the hamlet; and, as in the days
Of oracles each had its wonted shrine
And station, so old Robert did not lack
His proper tryst. A mighty old oak-tree
Within the park, fronting the far-off hills
That lay beyond the river, made for him,
Deep-hollowed close above its mossy roots,
A seat he loved. Here any one who sought
Would seek him when the sun was high at noon,
Or low at eve; but always he was there
At the first break of dawn, and hence it was
That, with a mingled reverence and jest,
They called him 'Morning Robert,' though his day
Was now far spent towards the eventide;
For a strange fancy took him in his age
Never to miss the sunrise any morn
The long year round. So, though at noon or eve
Perchance he wandered elsewhere, never came
The dawn in summer, autumn, winter, spring,

But found him underneath the old oak-tree
In vigil: there he saw the new day born
Above the hills, in clamour of the winds,
Or brooding mist, or rushing clouds of rain,
As in the still sweet air and silver sky.

  I held it dear to see and speak with him
Not seldom there. The picture as I came
Was worthy of remembrance—the great tree,
Knotted and gnarled with nigh a thousand years,
Yet wearing the new life of the last spring
Upon its summit greenly—underneath,
The old man seated, calm in that repose
Which is not of the world, with that child's look,
Most happy, blending with the dignity
Of many years and natural nobleness;
His long staff, reaching from him to the ground,
And on its end close clasped his wrinkled hands,
And over them the reverend reverent face;
The chin just laid upon the hand, the head
Leant back against the tree, and looking up,
Like hers, the saint of many tears and prayers—
Whom Scheffer drew—what time at Ostia
She sits with him, her son new born to God,
And communes with him of those future joys

Unseen, unknown, undreamed of, yet so near
They brighten o'er her!

       If he saw me come,
With honour for my office, and some love
(I love to think it) for me, he would rise,
And underneath his lifted hat reveal
The old man's 'crown of glory.' We would hold
That converse then which only they can hold
Who love one Lord; and, most of all, we dwelt
On the near glory of that heavenly day
For which, in night-time of the evil world,
God's people keep their vigil evermore.

 And yet, withal, there came to him no sign
That soon he should go hence, nor did he deem,
Despite his failing limbs and fourscore years,
His time was near, until, on one sad eve,
A little maiden whom he called 'Deare Childe,'
Making short sojourn in this pilgrim land,
Went home—went home, but left the world so dark
To us who loved her, and, not least, to him
To whose hoar winter she was like the spring,
So often that old tree was trysting-place
Where she would meet him after hours of school,
With sunbeams in her eyes and on her hair,

And merry prattle like the morning wind,
Or low sweet talk, like evening's softer breeze,
Of God, and heaven, and angels, and that Love
Which loved us unto death in Holy Land
Long years ago, and lives to love us still
Beyond the worlds.—Not till she passed away
He seemed to lose his vigorous hold on life;
But on that eve when, as the sun sank down,
Her soul arose and spread its wings for flight,
And left us to the darkness, as I went
Homeward, grief-stricken,—for I loved the child,
God knoweth!—leaning on the garden gate
I found him watching. With a single look
He read my wordless answer all too plain.
Perhaps a man's tears leave a deeper trace—
Perhaps some strange reflection, lingering still,
Caught from the deathly presence, told the tale—
Howbeit, he read it all, and turned away;
But such a groan broke from him, I was fain
To stay him with a hand upon his arm,
And force one word, 'The maiden is not dead,
But sleepeth.'
           Then he turned again and stood
Before me, silent. Neither spoke awhile,

And, though my grief was selfish, and I longed
To be alone with that remembered face,
That little form of saintly sweet repose,
And those last words, I might not leave him there,
So strangely grieved beyond the wont of age,
The whole frame rocked like some grey tower that feels
The earth-wave roll beneath it. So we stood;
The summer even darkening towards the night,
The breeze that rose at sunset from the west
Now dying wearily in sighs that shook
Faintly the leaves above us. Then again,
Touching his hand, I spoke. 'Is it too long
To tarry for the morning, when they meet
Who parted in the night? That morning comes
In God's good time; when He shall will it comes,
It will not tarry.' Then he raised his head
Quickly as one who hears, or thinks he hears,
A summons far away. A little while
He seemed as one who listened; then as though
He heard the voice that called him, 'Ah,' he said—
Musingly, not to me, within himself—
'The youngest, now the oldest.' Then a change
Revived the shaken frame, and lit the face,

Which had been dark, with light so strange and new,
I marvelled. But my own heart calling me
Back to myself, I left him with one word
Of benediction.
             But, from that day forth,
There was not one that might not mark a change
In Robert; not of weariness, or pain,
Or that which is the strength of many years,
'Labour and sorrow;' rather might be seen
A brightness, added to the wonted look
Of peace he wore. He did not seem like one
Waiting, however, patiently, for that
Which might be yet far off; but like a man
Who knows with joy one more swift hour will end
The long delay. It was, indeed, as though
Patience with him had had her perfect work,
And in his soul already had begun
The full joy of fruition. Yet to none
He bade Farewell. And some there were who said,
Noting that change which brightened in his face,
But seeing nought beneath it, 'Sure it was
Robert had got another lease of life,
And would outlive them all.' And others said,
'They marvelled Robert had so soon forgot

The little maid he seemed to dote upon.'
But those who knew him better saw the change,
And only wondered with a kind of awe.

But me he told in secret he believed
The time was very near when for his soul
The blessed dawn should break behind the hills,
And bring the eternal day. 'And yet,' he said,
'I do not know, sir, why I am so sure;
No angel told me; no, nor in a dream
Have I been warned; and so I do not say
Openly, I am sure, lest, if it be
I am mistaken, I should live to hear
My dear hope jested on—but, sir, I think
I cannot be mistaken, though no dream
Or angel has revealed it; for that night
On which the little maiden went to GOD,
And you, sir, told me, when my heart was sick,
That when the Lord shall will the morning comes
And will not tarry, then, I know not how,
But suddenly my breast was filled with joy,
As though I heard the footsteps of the Lord
Coming upon the mountains. "He will come,
He will not tarry," sounded in my soul;
Not faintly, as in whispers, but as though

A hundred voices said it. Then I thought,
Surely it is a message sent from God,
And by His priest He bids me stand prepared
For His quick coming. Therefore, sir, I wait,
Believing He is near. Yea, even so,
LORD JESUS, come! Amen.'
                              I looked at him,
His head bent low in utterance of the prayer,
The ancient, holy prayer, wherewith is closed
The great Apocalypse. And 'such,' I thought,
'Was he who prayed it on that latest page
Of inspiration, he, the most beloved
Where all were loved, yet last to pass away;
The old disciple, full of years, and worn
With many toils, but like a little child
In confidence and gentleness and love.'

  Summer was young when our 'deare childe' was
        laid
Under the chancel window, and her grave
Was still made bright, beneath the little cross,
With summer blossoms, when, one early morn,
I passed it by. No purpose led me forth,
Only a vague desire that I might feel

The first fresh breathing of the infant morn
And see its earliest smiling down the hills
And o'er the stream. I wandered by the wood,
And passed the lonely cottage. Then, I thought,
'Robert not yet has left his morning watch,
And he shall tell me with what joy he saw,
An hour ago, the sun rise.'

       From the wood
I came behind the tree to where he sat
Beneath it. Then I thought he was asleep,
Because he moved not, and his eyes, half-closed,
Seemed overcast and dim, and when I spoke
He did not hear me.

      'Robert! do you sleep?'
I said, and bent to touch him.—Then I saw
Indeed he slept. It was the sleep of him
Who slept within the cave of Bethany,
Whom none could wake but Jesus.

        He was dead:
Dead underneath the dying old oak tree—
(Its last leaf died that autumn). 'O my friend,'
I cried, with tearless bitterness at heart,
'I came to hear thee speak of light and joy,
And thou art dead!'

                    Shivering with grief, I turned,
And—lo! before me glowed the living Morn—
The great unclouded Sun above the hills
Made hills and woods and river beautiful;
And overhead, unseen, I just might hear
A lark that sang to God his matin song
Of praise for light and joy.
                              Again I turned,
Fronting the sleeping saint, and as my tears
Fell part in sorrow, part in penitence,
I knelt beside him with that ancient prayer,
As I had heard him pray it, 'Even so,
LORD JESUS, come! Amen.'
                         Thus did he die,
That good old man. And for ourselves, indeed,
It could not be but we must mourn for him.
We miss him at the solitary tree;
We miss his reverent greeting by the way;
We miss him in the Church's holy hours
From that grey pillar, and the Altar-rail.
How many mourn that childless, poor old man!
That lonely, unimportant, poor old man!
Oh, nay!—that heir of heaven, that royal saint,
That brother of the LORD, that king and priest

To God Almighty! Yes, and we who mourn
With love's true sorrow, yet will never say
'Alas!' but 'Hallelujah!'—lost to us,
But found in heavenly places! He has left
A vacant niche in earth's cathedral front,
But in God's Eden, by the crystal stream,
Under the tree of life, a glorious form,
He fills a glorious place; his eyes behold
The Great King in His beauty; in the glow
And splendour of that Day, for which he looked
And longed and waited, now at last he hears
The chantings of the myriad morning stars
Of which he caught the echoes, though so far
Not faintly, here.

     For us, who still are here,
We follow: if so be, by grace of Christ,
We also may attain, and hear, like him,
The Voice of the Beloved, beyond the hills,
Calling our souls to gather to His light,
When the day breaks, and shadows flee away.

III.

The Quest of Love.

A PARISH IDYLL.

'The love of things created endureth not; the love of Jesus is faithful.'
THOMAS À KEMPIS.

HIS was a tale of twenty years ago:
    Never forgotten, told and told again
To his indignant heart, in every pause
Between the changes of a restless life
Self-exiled to the East; a memory
Of man's ill-will and woman's broken faith
Like a perpetual discord, never mute,
But marring all the music in the world,
A ghostly dismal shriek, for ever heard
Amid its kindliest laughter.
                      Time had been
When the pure waters of his heart, which now
Were bitter as the sea of death, had flowed
Fresh as a river of Eden, overshone

By every gracious light, and breathed upon
By all the winds of hope.

      An only son
Left motherless so young, he scarcely knew,
As days sped on, whether the gentle face
He summoned up so often was the work
Of memory or fancy—till his years
Had reached a double decade Leonard lived
With stern Sir Hugh, his father, in the house,
Half house, half ruin, on a wooded hill
Behind the Squire's great hall. Its ancient name
Clung to it, and although the spacious lands,
Its heritage for twice three hundred years,
All save a few poor fields had passed away,
Now for a generation, to the hands
Of that new lord the Squire, the country folk
Still named 'The Castle' with a tender pride,
And gave a readier reverence to Sir Hugh
Despite his broken fortunes than to him
Who built the new great palace in the park;
'Although,' said they, 'he is a kindly man,
And you'll not find in all the country round
A better master; but the good old blood
Flows where it flowed and is not bought with gold

And we had liefer serve the ancient race
Our fathers loved and served a thousand years.'
   Fain would the Squire have joined good heart and
      hand
With Leonard's father, had he willed, but he,
Wrathfully brooding on the wrongs of fate—
So did he phrase his own sire's thriftlessness—
Swore never to set foot within the hall
Of this usurper of his heritage,
And met the other's readiest courtesies
With nothing save a gesture or a word
Of coldest salutation.
                    But his son,
Just as the breezy morning of his youth
Was merging into noon, and in his heart
The first soft breathing of a warmer wind
Prefaced the way for love, and heralded
With inarticulate sweet whisperings
Some near mysterious advent, by a chance—
By both kept secret in a mutual fear—
Met the one daughter of the Squire. No need
To say how this befel, and how his hand
Saved her from peril: how they met again,
And yet again a hundred times, till Love

Revealed himself, and solved the mystery,
The sweet vague expectation of the noon,
And in the power of his apocalypse
Swallowed up life and changed the world to him:
All things were made for Love, so truly Love's
That Love was all, the world had nothing else
But Love.

   And so one summer day (alas!
How black is tempest on a summer day),
Subduing all mistrust, with happy tears
Of blissful triumph in his earnest eyes,
He told Sir Hugh his secret. His were met
With eyes to which the bitter brooding fiend,
That in his heart like levin in the cloud
Had lain so long, sprang with a fire of wrath
Deadlier to hope that e'en the furious words
Which followed like quick thunder.

    'Boy,' he cried,
'But dare to see this upstart once again
And I will curse you every wretched hour
Until I die.'

   Through all the bygone years,
Leonard remembered how Sir Hugh, so stern
And sad to others, had been good to him

And gracious, watching him with silent pride
As if he verily loved him. And so then,
When horror and amazement spared him words,
He prayed his father, by the memory
Of what he deemed had been his love for him,
To give him were it but one word of hope
And pity; or, indeed, if he had sinned,
Of pardon; then, unheeded, passionately
Sinking upon his knees, he cried, 'Oh, sir,
By my dead mother!' But the fierce old man,
Stung to yet fiercer wrath, ere he could end
His prayer, broke in, thrust back his clinging hands,
And spurned him, vowing by the eternal God
Of dead and living that it should not be,
Were it to save his own life or bring back
That mother from the dead!

       Then Leonard rose
Without another word, and, with a heart
In which new anguish battled with old love
And tore his father's image from its shrine
And trampled on it, down the park he raged,
And burst upon the astonished Squire, and cried
'Oh, sir, I have no father and no home!
Give me your daughter, and be this my home,

And you my father!'
               But the kindly man,
When Leonard gathered breath and told him all,
Grew wroth in turn, and sware no child of his
Should wed with one whose father came not there
To sue for her right humbly.
                    Late that night
Sir Hugh's old servant, sent to seek for him,
Found him beneath a cypress in the dell
Stretched out, and still as death, and thought him dead,
But his great cry of fear awoke the lad,
On whom, worn out with passion, God had sent
Only day's death of sleep.
                    A month at home
He watched his father's altered countenance,
Who only spoke to ask him, 'Have you yet
Forgot your folly?' and was answered 'No.'
  Then thought Sir Hugh, 'Here will he pine, for here
There is no stir nor change to break the spell:
He shall go hence, to find in busier scenes
Some better food for fancy.' Thereupon
He sent him wandering over half the world
Two years—but ere the second year was dead

Came Death to him, and on that stern sad heart
Suddenly laid his hand. And Leonard came,
Summoned in haste a thousand leagues away;
Two passions, diverse fruits of love, at war
Within his breast,—true grief for him whom death
Absolved from that past bitterness, and hope,
Bright Hope, that waved back sorrow at the bier,
And said, 'Give place, the barrier falls, and Love—
Love that was let so long—is come again
At last to have his will and claim his own.'
Alas! how false was hope! He came to find
That there was deeper anguish in the world
Than he had known; a bitterer draught of pain
Set for his lips; a cruel hand to smite
Deeper into his life than that dead man's.

   It is soon said. Her whom his hand had saved,
Her for whose sake he would have given his soul
Surrendering heaven as he surrendered home,
Her whom his arms had held the while in tears
Her low voice sware beneath the linden tree,
Between his kisses that fair summer eve,
That she was his for ever—her he found
A wife, another's, aye, a willing wife!—
No forced possession but a willing wife,

Who, when, refusing to believe, he came
Before her, lifting up her languid eyes
Smiled slowly on him, 'hoped they might be friends
Despite that youthful folly which no doubt
He almost had forgotten!'
       Not one word
He gave her, only from a ghastly face
One look—but one—and yet her smile fell dead,
And she grew white with fear.
        Back to the shore
From which so late the wings of love and hope
Had borne him, he returned—despair and hate,
His sole familiar friends—an infidel
Of love and so of heaven. So sped his life,
Most desolate and forlorn, a living death,
For eighteen years; and then he wandered back
Slowly, like one obedient to a power
He wots not of, back to the home where once
He had believed in love, and, as he deemed,
In heaven.
    Awhile he kept himself apart
Within the ancient castle, now still more
A ruin, like his life; but afterwards
He wandered to and fro among the scenes

Of those first innocent years.
                        That year was young;
Not many weeks had her Evangelist
Of resurrection, Spring, whose angel feet
Are beautiful in Winter's wilderness,
Been whispering glad tidings of new life
To wood and field and hedgerow,—yet they wore
The robes of their redemption from the doom
And death of winter. 'Singing robes' were they,
Clothing the grandest bard, the poet of God,
Nature, who sang the song of her deep heart,
The song of never-dying life and love,
In every branch and flower.
                        Was this the spell
That drew him forth one noon a longer way?
Howbeit, that noon his lonely, listless feet
Beyond the wonted limit wandered on,
Until he reached the old grey churchyard wall,
And leaned upon the little gate and mused.
''Tis here,' he said, 'in yonder church she sleeps,
My mother; on her tomb her own last words
Said, so they tell, o'er my unconscious head
In dying benediction, "God is love."
And here I stand, her son, so near her tomb,

To doubt of God as I do doubt of love.
And yet, none doubted of her love, they say,
And me, too young for doubt or for belief,
Better than life she loved. I have disproved
All else but that. God! if there be a God,
Reveal Thyself! O Love, if Thou art Love,
Send me some sign, some messenger! this doubt,
Most hateful as it is the fruit of hate,
Is hell.'

   So passionately in thought he cried
Then on a sudden marvelling at himself,
He mocked his aspiration with a laugh
Of helpless, hopeless, melancholy scorn
At his own soul in prayer.

      And then again,
His bitter musings, in their wonted tide,
One after one rolled in upon his mind,
Like salt waves plunging on a frozen shore,
With not one raindrop of a softer sorrow
To mingle with the brine, nor yet a sigh
Of that low wind whose breathing is as sweet
With tender memories and with trustful hopes
As it is sad with loss: no wind like this,
Only the wrathful east, that never thaws

The frozen depth of tears.

                      And all the while,
Leaning upon the gate and motionless,
He did not mark a little maiden's form
Behind him, still, and waiting patiently—
With wistful eyes as sunny sweet as morn,
And coloured like the violets in her hand,—
A little maiden hardly seven years old,
But with a face so pure and fair, you thought
That her own angel which in heaven beheld
The FATHER's face could scarcely be more fair.

  At last he heard her plaintive 'Oh sir, please—'
And turning listlessly as one in sleep
Upon whose ears an unfamiliar voice
Falls, and he does not heed, yet opens wide
His slumber-laden eyes, and gazes round
On him who speaks, but does not say one word
Nor truly seem to see: so now he turned
An unregarding look upon the child,
Whose wide-eyed wonder would have grown to fear
At this great barrier which still kept the way
Despite her pleading, and gazed down on her
So strangely—save that fear of any man
In all her bright young life had never come

To fling on her one shadow of mistrust.
And so she did not doubt or shrink, although
She very greatly wondered. Then, again,
She said, beseeching, 'Please, sir, may I pass?'
Whereat he rose, and, like a man whose dream
Suddenly melts away, he saw the child
How fair she was—and thinking in his heart
'Is this my messenger?' put out his arm
And stayed her as she passed him, saying, 'Child,
Tell me whence came you with your flowers?' And
    she,
Lifting her sunny eyes, replied, 'From home.'
Then added, when she saw he waited still,
'Where father lives, the shepherd; every one
Knows father.'
        'And the violets, little maid?'
'For him,' she said, and pointed past the church
To where the rectory lay amid the trees.
  'Why do you take them?' said he.
                'Sir, because
He loves me and he loves the flowers.'
                                He asked,
'And you, you love him?'
                     'I; Oh yes,' she cried,

'Of course I love him—father loves him too,
And mother.'
    'Why?' he said; and she, 'Oh sir,
Because he loves us, and he talks to us
Of things we love.'
    'What things, my maid?' 'Oh sir,
Numbers of happy things.'
    'But tell me them,
These happy things.'
    'They are so many, sir;
For some of them he tells to us at home,
And some at school, and some—'
    And here her voice
Grew lower, not less happy, though more grave—
'And some, sir, there,'—turning her look away,
Where, old indeed but beautiful in age,—
In earthly place, yet pointing heavenward,—
Lay in the clear noonlight the village Fane.
A lowly shrine, yet no mean type of Her,
The great Church-Mother, blessing the whole world,
While looking for that Other and her Lord.
 'And what,' he asked her, 'does he tell you there
You love to hear?'
    'He tells us most of all,

For that is best of all—we love it best—
Of JESUS.'

    Here she bowed her little head,
And the great NAME went whispered through her lips
Spoken as if she stood on holy ground,
And in a sacred Presence: yet as if
Holy was happy, Sacred sweet to her.
 He stood a moment silent; then he said,
'Child, tell me why that is the best of all
Those happy things you hear? what has He done
That you should think it best?'

      'Oh sir, you know
He loved us, and He died upon the Cross,
Because He loved us so.'

     'What made you sure
This tale is true?'

    'Oh sir, it must be true.
The Bible says it; and how else could we
Love Him so dearly?'

     'And can I, too, learn
Such Love as this?' he said.

      Up in his face
She looked with timid eyes he could not meet.
And said, 'He loved you and He died for you.

Oh, *don't* you love Him!'

       'Teach me, little child,
To love Him.'

      While he spoke his eyes were dim,
So dim he could not see her as she stood
And took his hand to draw him and replied,
'Oh sir, I am so little: only come
Over the churchyard there and speak to him,
And he will teach you.'

      But he started back,
Like one who breaks a spell; and as ashamed
Of weakness which had caught him unawares,
He dropped her hand, and muttering scornfully,
'No priests for me,' he turned as if to go,
Saying, 'I will not.'

      But she said again,
Most wistfully, 'Oh come, sir, please to come!'
And so he turned, and met the pleading eyes.
Ah, blessed Spirit of love! the pitiful God—
Who would not lose his soul, so sad and blind,
So longing and forlorn—was in her face,
And moved a will which had been stubborn still,
Though all the banded strength of all the world
Had wrestled with it. For that golden age,

Whose grace far off the Son of Amoz saw
And sang, flings even now from time to time,
Aye, day by day, some sign upon the world
That it is surely coming : and the wolf,
The leopard, and the lion in the wilds,
Forego their nature, quit their kind,—and lo !
A little child doth lead them. Even so
She won him from the waste wherein so long
His heart had wandered in its hate and scorn :
Won him with simple words and tender trust,
And littleness of guile,—so weak, so strong :
So strong in weakness ; he so weak in strength ;
She knew so little, he so much, of life ;
Truly she knew so little ; but she knew
Of Love, and Love is all ; and with the cords
Of Love she drew him.

      'Come, sir ! please to come !'
He stooped, and took her in his arms, and said,
'This is my messenger, and I will go.'
Then said no more, but as a man who knows
His purpose may not hold, pressed quickly on.
And she, Deare Childe, well pleased that he should go,
And pleased to find herself perched up so high
Upon his shoulder, prattled as they went,

Nor knew she was an angel sent from God,—
An angel sent to win a soul from death,
And baffle the proud fiend that rules the world,—
Prattled about the violets, and said,
She had been up that day at early dawn,
And gone with 'Morning Robert' to the dell
That hides itself behind the little lake,
And there had found the flowers;

       'And, sir,' she said,—
'If once you come within the dell, you know
The flowers are there, although you never look
To find them, for they fill the air with scent;
They grow so thick and smell so sweet.'

          But now,
Ere he had said another word, they stood
Before the garden gate; and from the porch,
Beneath whose honeysuckle eaves I sat,
I saw them. From my book I rose, and came
To meet them, wondering where my little maid
Had found this strange companion on her way
To bring her wonted offering of the flowers:
Herself the rarest and least earthly flower
Of that dear garden of the Church of God,—
The desert world's oasis—where my Lord

To work for Him awhile, to train and tend,
Hath set me.
                    Seeing me he lifted down
His burden: but he would not let her go,
But kept her by the hand, as one who holds
By some last hope, not surely, yet full well
Knowing it is the last.   Then, as I came,
Said, 'Wherefore I am come, sir, scarce I know;
Perchance for nothing; yet, if there be Love,
For more than I have found in all the world:
Yet whether this or that, for nought or all,
I surely had not troubled you, except
This little child had led me.'
                                While he spake
I saw his face was noble; somewhat hard,
Yet not as if it had been always hard:
A high, broad forehead over hazel eyes
Clear, keen, and cold; the mouth was beautiful,
Save for a touch of scorn or hopelessness
As sad as death: yet, as with his last words,
He glanced a moment at the child, there came
Over the eyes and mouth a sudden gleam
That seemed to show his mother in the man,
Which faded as he drew his glance away

And fronted mine, and left him, as at first,
Half scornfully, half diffidently, cold,
And listlessly expectant.
      But the child,
Ere I could answer, ran to me and said—
Whispering as I bent to take the flowers,—
'He wants to hear of Him Who loved us so
And died for us.'
      I kissed her, with a prayer,
Deep in my startled soul, for such a power
As hers of love to speak on such a theme.
And then she turned to him and raised her face—
Sweet, purely child-like, peaceful, confident,
And yet so meekly wistful—up to him,
And waited till he kissed her—then she went.

 I said, 'She is so little and so young,
And only just so learned that she can read;
And I have faced the world for fifty years,
And studied in the books and hearts of men,
And fought the battle of life with foes without
And dreader foes within: yet, well I know
She is more learn'd than I; and her white soul
Reflects the truth and light and love of God
For better teaching to your need; and I—

I falter now that you should come from her
To me. Can I not see that even now
Your eyes are colder and your face more hard
Since she is here no longer? I avow
That were it not my pledge to Him Who gave
This office holds me, and my trust is large
That He will speak by one whom He hath sent
And will not fail me, I would say, Go back:
Sit at her feet, and from her baby lips
Shall the great Lord of wisdom and of love
Perfect His praise.

              Yet doubt not of my faith:
For, oh, my friend, I do believe in Love,
And Him Who is the whole of Love to me:
And I whose life, despite this peaceful eve,
Has been no summer day, but wild and dark,—
After the blithest morn and brightest noon,—
Am not less sure of such a grace for you;
That you, who found no love in all the world,
May find in Him what shall suffice for all
Past loss and future need; aye, more, and give
A beauty, such as only comes from Heaven,
To all things earthly; not a mere content
And patience, but a beauty and a joy,

Making you glad to live.'
　　　　　　　　　Deep was the night
Before we parted; and he went his way
Under a still dark sky that watched for morn,
And through the woods wherein the new spring life
Seemed yearning in the silence as in prayer.

　He left me with few words, yet these, the best,
That he would come again.
　　　　　　　　　Again he came,
And often; and at first, almost like one
Unmoved, he listened, for he gave no sign;
Yet had I hope, because he seemed to hear
And sought to stay. Then, after many days,
There came a change, as if the spirit of ill
Suddenly rose within him in great wrath,
Knowing his time was short. He set his soul
Fiercely in battle array, and hurled his darts,
Tipped with fine scorn, at every point, and watched
With eager, desperate eyes, as if the hour
Now were supreme for some full end. Anon
The fiend departed, leaving him half dead.
Not doubt now held him, but despair; and Love
Seemed but too real, too high a heavenly flower
For him to reach and gather, and to wear

On such a heart alien so long. I said,
'The love of Christ is depth as well as height;
It leaneth down so low to raise so high.
None lie so low, save those who will not heed,
But in the darkness they may find His hand,
And hear the calm, profound, pathetic Voice,
"Come unto Me. Deep was Gethsemane,
And Calvary dark,—did I not love thee? Come."'
 But he would lay his head upon his hand,
With only this: 'Too late! it is too late.'

 So the days sped. Spring passed, and in her place
Stood the imperial summer thrice as fair;
Yet was there, ere she came, one awful hour,
Brief but tremendous; such a storm it seemed,
As if the wintry spirits that yet lurked
In nature gathered in their parting hour
To tear the world.
     That night he stood and watched
At the wide window of his ancient house
The writhing woods and rushing broken heaven.
 Then, as the darkness and the conflict grew
Deeper and wilder, on his soul there fell
A light and calm.

                        At first he did not dare
To trust it; but it grew—the light more clear,
The calm more deep: no sudden ecstacy
Or rapture was it, but a still repose,
The strength of quietness and confidence
Stronger than passion.
                        Louder roared the storm,
And thicker fell the darkness. Then he knelt,
And with full eyes, that saw not the near storm,
But far away the perfect peace, he prayed,
'So late, so late, yet bless me! I believe,
LORD JESUS, I believe in Love and Thee!'

And so—while thus in legion from the woods
The winds, like evil angels mad with loss,
Rushed with ten thousand shrieks and beat themselves,
As in a vain despair, against the walls—
Past that black night, up to the awful Throne,
Through all the pealing praise of myriad worlds,
Sped that low prayer; and round about the throne
And through all infinite spaces of the heavens,
The holy angels heard it and looked down;
And lo! the rapture of their endless song
Caught a new note—joy for another soul

Won to the blest obedience of Love,
The kingdom and the glory of the Lamb.

. . . . . .

But ah, my little maid, my little maid!
I end, who tell this tale, with other tears
Than those of joy—the joy before my God
Of those who bring the golden harvest home—
With other tears for thee. That night came down
A messenger to warn us that the King
Had need of her whom He had given awhile;
And ere a week He called her.
       Do I sin
In sorrow for her gain? Pardon me this,
LORD, if I sin. I know it is her gain.
Her single hour of labour light was done,
And now—like one at even after school
Beside a Father's feet—she sits at Home,
Deare Childe, beholding Him, Whom, seeing not,
She loved so well, believing. 'Tis her gain.
But ah, my desolate garden! there are flowers,
Yet many, that I love; but none like thee,
Not one, my little maid, my little maid.

IV.

The Rectory Farm.

A PARISH IDYLL.

IN TWO PARTS.

PART I.

THE little hamlet lies within the vale
    One side the winding river, yet it seems
To hanker for the uplands. Here and there
A cottage flings its shade upon the stream:
And on the level narrow length, that makes
A sandless emerald shore by saltless waves,
Thatched roofs in clusters at wide intervals
Break up a mile of greensward: but behind
Begins the slope that finds its wooded crown
On lowly hills some half a league away;
And on this slope, in groups of three or four,
Or single, half a hundred cottages,
White walled, dark roofed, and mostly bowered in
    green,

Seem creeping upwards, higher still and higher,
But in a lessening order, till at last,
Highest of all but yet below the wood,
An ancient church, square-towered and ivy-clad,
Stands in God's Acre. On its western side,
And near the border wall of mossy stone,
A yew tree planted when the church was young,
Nor now less fair for its five hundred years
Than the old reverend fane, across the wall
Thrusts out one mighty arm which casts a shade
Upon the pathway, by a garden lawn
That runs all edged with barricades of bloom,
And sentinelled with lindens all its length
In broken order, over a broad wall
Of laurels and arbutes.
     Beyond the lawn
The Rectory, shaded by a group of elms,
Lies like a bower of rest, though not of art
Or splendour. Quaint and old, its gabled front,
Behind a porch with honey-suckle eaves,
Looks out of depths of ancient ivy here,
And there of jasmine. Through the elms behind
The higher casements eastward overlook
Far off the parted river's silver sheen

Below the weir, and, past the stream, the hills
Against the morning heavens. But toward the west
Is meadow-land 'twixt leafy lanes ; and last
A Farm, beneath a sloping wood that moves
Still further westward till it lies a gloom
Against the autumn sunsets.
                            Chief of all
That lay dispread at spacious intervals
About the church, and nearest, this was hight
The Rectory Farm.
                    A goodly home was this
Of a long line of yeomen : old and new ;
Old—for the mighty timbers and strong walls
Cried shame on the frail work of later thrift ;
New—for an ever watchful eye, and hands
That ever wrought amain, had checked decay ;
Nor was there lack within of modern art
For grace or comfort, apt appliances
To meet all daily needs of hand or head
For work or leisure. Not the Squire's great Hall—
For all its costlier splendours and new stores
Of ever-added over-crowded means
Of luxury and ornament—nor yet
The Castle—yonder on the wooded height,

All bare of splendour, but a reverend place
With ancient chambers tapestried and dim,
Half house, half ruin, once the stern Sir Hugh's,
Now 'sad Sir Leonard's,' (so they called his son,
A lonely man)—nor this nor that could boast
More prosperous aspect or securer weal,
A brighter comfort, a more genial board,
Or more of all that serves a ready will
To give good welcome to as many friends
As might deserve to claim it.
      Farmer Leigh
Looked down upon the Squire, despite his lands
And all that wealth which fame made ever more;
Was not his house by these three hundred years
More ancient than the Hall? and though he looked
Still with the wonted reverence of his race
Up to the Castle, yet withal he knew
Himself was wealthier than had been Sir Hugh
Or was Sir Leonard.
      But there came a day
So dark—made all the home he loved so well
So desolate—he sat within a broken man,
Nor could for woe look elsewhere up or down.

A strange intruder at the Rectory Farm
Was trouble: and because he was so strange
The more unwelcome. Those who know him best
Look at him with less fear, if they have learnt
Aught of his office, trusting once again
That they may find some love within his eyes,
Which seem at first to wither all the bloom
They rest on—still may find him as of old,
Ever no tyrant though so stern and sad:
A Teacher rather, in whose sombre school
Is surely taught, to hearts that will to learn,
The way of peace but seldom known or found
By Pleasure's pupils.
     Farmer Leigh was rich:
With many a treasure in his house and field
He held right dear: whereon he fed his pride,
Till it waxed fat and grew beyond control
To an imperious fullness that would brook
Let of his will from none.
      But one there was
Of all his treasures—house, and lands, and stores,
Laid up for many years, his friends and kin
Who gave him worship, or his five strong sons,
Worthy their name—one was there of them all

A hundred times the dearest. Had he been
Without another treasure in the world,
Saving this one, forlorn—no whit the more
Would she have been within his heart of hearts
His one ewe lamb.
     His daughter: not alone
A present joy, and dear to his proud hope,
But for one memory dearer; to his eyes
Restoring her dead mother.
      Ten years back
She was the prettiest child in all the shire,
And now the fairest woman. Form and face,
If ever such a word befits this world,
Were faultless. Dark-eyed, like the moonless night
The stars make softly splendid: with such hair
As would itself have made a woman's fame:
Quick-brained, large-hearted, with a poet's soul
Of passionate force: withal being pure and true,
She lacked no pearl of loveliness and grace,
Save one—but 'tis the one white pearl of all.
Drawn from the deep, and therefore of the height,
Priceless, because it is of price in Heaven
Saith the Apostle: Mary's ornament,
'A meek and quiet spirit.'

'Twas not Kate's ;
Nor was her father's that which makes a man
Greatest: in lack of which, however strong,
No man, when need is sorest, overcomes:
The wisdom that controls the manly will,'
The calm and earnest heart that knows itself,
And owns a law, not seeking what it can,
But what it may, and, patient in its strength,
Still in its strong persistence can forbear.
  So was it that between these loving hearts
And noble natures ebbed and flowed a tide
Of discord: he, exacting all his will ;
She, unsubmissive, or beneath the yoke
Vexed and impatient.
                    But there came a day
When discord grew to ruin in an hour ;
Then died between them in the shadow of death.
  Long had the village marvelled such a maid—
Proud as she was, 'she had a heart,' they said—
Was yet unwon: for many a wooer came
From near and far, of good report, but all
Upon a fruitless quest. For there was one
Whom she had slowly learned from childish years—
Slowly, but surely, to the height and depth

Of her large nature—learned to love. But he—
Though else all worthy, for the grace and strength
Of more than all his manly comeliness
Broadened his brow and deepened in his smile—
Was poorer, though of distant kin to them,
And knew himself to be her father's fear,
Who wished a wealthier lover for his maid,
And set his will against him watchfully.

  And so long while he did not tell his love,
So vexing her, whose pride was all aglow.
And when at length he spoke, she put him off
With such a seeming ease, his earnest heart
Made sure she did not love him.

                                  But at last,
Because she had been kinder than her wont,
(Fain and more fain her heart to smile on him,)
And since his love was such, his lonely home
Were he unloved, could be his home no more,
He spoke again—meeting her as he rode
One even by the orchard wall, and there
Dismounting spoke, and as a man should speak,
With tender grave devotion, honouring her
E'en as he loved her, wholly, but not less
Honouring his word, and speaking once for all.

Then rose that lurking devil of her pride,
And said within her, 'Test him, let him sue
And serve yet longer, till you give him all.'
And so she checked the angel of her joy
That sang within, and let that imp of hell
Speak falsely for her, with uncertain words
Of trifling. But he stayed her, and replied:
'Kate, it is once for all: there is my horse;
If you can ever love me, bid me stay;
If not, and you would have me dead to you,
Say "Go," and you shall never see me more.'

She in her sin made answer, 'You may go;'
And in the moment's madness laughed at him:
Then, the next instant, glancing at his face,
She saw it wan like death, and grew herself
So sick at heart with love and some strange fear,
She could have knelt to stay him, but his woe
Blinded him, and he turned and rode away.

Blindly he rode—for this was bitter woe,
More than love's loss; 'twas hard indeed to lose,
But not to honour her whom he had lost!
There was a woe in this that wrung his soul,
And dazed him, that he knew not how he rode,
And, ere he reached his home, his headlong horse

Stumbled, and fell, and rolled ; then rose again
Without his master.
                    She, when he was gone,
Heart-sick at first, remembering that last look,
Went slowly home, but rallied from her fear ;
And then, poor fool ! began to soothe her soul
With happy visions—Soon would he return,
And nevermore would she be cold again,
But give him tenderest homage, heart and will ;
Sweet would it be to tell him all her love
With joy and reverence—that she only lived
To love and serve him !
                    So she mused, and night
Fell : and her musings passed into her dreams :
And he lay dying.

PART II.

            At his side I watched,
For he had been in Christ a son to me,
Revered as well as loved through many a year
Of steadfast life in God.
                    The long night passed

In stupor: but at morning he awoke,
Painless but near to death. In peaceful awe
He lay and waited, while I spoke or prayed;
Then came the mystic Feast of Life in Death—
Then his soul passed at noon.

       But ere the end
He told me all—the hopes of all his youth,
And how they closed; then, when I asked of him
If he forgave—'Forgive?' he said; 'O Sir,
I love, I love her! Oh, that she would come
And hear me say I love her: and perchance—
Even if she love me not—because I go
She will forgive my love, and as I go
Will pray God bless me.'

       Hearing him, I sent
One who might bring her, would she come: but he
Returning said, her father, whom he saw,
Brought answer from his daughter from within—
'The tidings grieved her, but she could not come.'

 And so he died: nor knew her love, nor knew
The answer was not hers, but falsely sent
By that infatuate slave of his own will,
In fear that, if the sick man did not die,
Such piteous meeting at the gates of death

Would make her his for life.

       O fool! he lied,
Nor thought he lied, but only held his will.
 And her no tidings reached long past the noon:
And all her thoughts were his, and all were sweet,
Save that vague fear and that remembered look.
And thus in tender musing, as the day
Drew softly on to even, down the path
Beside the orchard wall she wandered on
Alone, and longing for his face again.

 'Tis writ, 'At evening time it shall be light;'
So shall it be, so is it, to the just,
The meek in spirit and the true of soul,
Strong against trouble in the quietness
Of holy trust; but to the froward heart,
Whose peace is the idolatrous repose
Of sated pride—Self set on high and crowned,
And fed with worship—at the evening time
Rather God's blasting levin than the light
And glory of His grace, and afterward
Blackness of darkness. Holy is His NAME,
GOD of all mercies, yet the Jealous GOD.

  There, as she mused and longed, broke on her
    dream

The voice of one who, passing, told her all—
One of his kin who loved him, hating her
For what she deemed had been her scorn of him—
Told her of that blind ride away from her,
And of his hurt to death; then cried at last
With passionate speech, which shook as a dart shakes
That through the hissing air goes quivering home:—
'Yes, he is dead! you beautiful bad girl!
I tell you he is dead, and you have done it:
And—oh, your hard heart!—as he lay a-dying
He cried for you, just for one look, one word;
Might he but see you once before he died,
Might he but say once more, "I love you, Kate;
Will you not say 'God bless you!' since I go
And shall not vex you longer?" So he cried:
And you, you, you—you send to him and say
You will not! Oh! I looked upon his face,
And saw it change and ashen as he heard,
And turned him to the wall, and sighed, "My God,
Bless her I love, who loves me not." I looked,
And thought, for all it is his dying prayer,
And he a godly man, God will not hear it:
What! God send blessing down on *you* from Heaven!
God let *you* see him in that other world!

To make perchance a mock again of love
So wasted on your hard hard heart! Oh, you!
Remorseless—you may laugh beside his grave,
If so you will, one day, but that is all!
For you shall never never see him more.'

   More had she said, but something made her pause
That came upon her from the awful face
Before her—not of words, for it was still
And set, as some grey marble agony—
Something of passion greater than her own
Which paled before it like a lifted torch
Under a burning mountain. So she turned
And went her way—but afterward she said
That, looking back a moment on the girl,
She saw her lift her arms and make a cry—
A sob, or cry—and turning suddenly
Speed homewards.

                Home she went, all wildly crazed
With love's despair, and hatred worse than death
Against her father. With low shuddering sighs,
As one half conscious, of those bitter words
The first and last repeating, '*He is dead,
And you shall never never see him more,*'
She went from room to room in the still house,

Nor found him or her brethren; then awhile
Sat, while the evening fell, nor ever ceased
The woeful iteration; till at last,
As one who, hopeless on a hateful way,
Suddenly sees an end and welcomes it,
Nor knows nor cares save that it is an end,
She started, rose, and, where her father's eye
Would surely find them, left these written words,
'*I have killed him: I have lost him: he is dead,*
And I shall never never see him more.
And you have killed us both, for I must die.
Since I have killed him, I will kill myself:
I have lost him and my soul—for he is dead,
And I shall never never see him more.'

Then from the house she passed, and took her way,
All slowly now, now madly in all haste,
Through the long meadows that beneath the woods
Slope toward the vale. Not yet she sought the vale,
Shunning the scattered hamlet, but pressed on
Where, past the Park, there lies an open wold,
Of every dwelling save a sheep-fold bare,
Whence, seen of none, she thought to reach the vale.
But ere she touched the wold she came on one—
Hard by a single cottage 'neath the eaves

Of the last wood below the furthest hill—
No spirit, yet an angel. God the Lord
Not only once hath set a little child
In midst of His disciples, saying, 'Lo,
The greatest in My kingdom.'

                          In the lane,
Returning from the shepherd on the wold,
Home ere the night should fall, there met the girl
This heavenly messenger in lowly form,
A little maiden. Known and loved was she—
'Deare Childe' of our election over all
To the wide hamlet: such a grace was in her,
It needed not her loveliness to win
Our tender homage; and to Kate more dear
For six years memory of a sister dead,
Whose name she bore.

                     Yet now she had not stayed
For even a word or glance, save that the child
Ran to her gladly, looking in her face
For the familiar greeting, and saw there
So wild a horror, that she hid her own
In the girl's dress, and clasped her with her arms,
And cried, 'O Kate, O Kate!'—but she, all dazed,
Still to herself repeating, 'He is dead,

And I shall never never see him more,'
Gave her no heed, till once again the child
Lifting her face, but clinging closer, cried—
Scarce knowing what she said, but saying that
The childly instinct taught her—'Kate, O Kate,
I love you!'

    At the words, since they had been
His words, the girl, starting as one who hears
Or seems to hear an utterance of the dead,
Tore herself from the child, and thrust her back.
Then turned as if for flight; but turned again,
And took her in her arms all terrified,
Kissing her wildly; then without a word,
Loosing her strange embrace and leaving her,
Fled down the wold.

    A mile, like one pursued,
She swiftly sped: then at the borders fell,
And lay upon her face among the ferns,
Scarce conscious, but not ceasing still to cry,
'Dead, dead: and I shall never see him more:'
But now upon the cry—as on a curse
Follows remission—in her ears the words,
By grace of God remembered, '*Kate, O Kate,
I love you!*' followed. Then she rose again

And staggered through the vale beside the stream,
And reached the house where her dead lover lay.
O then the curse revived! and since she knew
He lay within, and could not speak to her,
And could not say he loved her, or forgave,
But lay there dead—for ever dead to her—
She straight had died—beat out her hateful life
Against those funeral walls, or cast herself
Into the still deep stream—save that again,
Upon that iteration, ' Nevermore,'
Fell, charm-like still, the blessing, '*Kate, O Kate,
I love you—love you;*' and she paused to hear.

So did she stand, as one beside a tomb:
Near, and so far: near, not a rood from her,
Lay all her world; so far, between them spread
Eternal distance! Then once more her heart,
Heaving in throes of tearless agony,
Drove her to flight. 'Away from him,' she thought,
'And I may die.' And down the darkling stream
She sped, nor paused till on the bridge she heard
The ceaseless ominous murmur of the fall
Plunging in the abysmal pool.
       She stood
Over the middle arch : listened and stood;

The night wind moaning round her, and the weir
Calling before her 'neath its ghostly veil:
Listened, as one who listens for a sign.
  Terrible night—it wore a look more fell
Because it was not wild: there were no shrieks
Of wrathful or tormented winds to seem
In sympathy with her despairing soul,
And so to soothe her; no impetuous floods,
Like the great deep of passion broken up,
Forcing relief; not even a few still tears
Of rain, to whisper her poor heart that heaven
Was weeping for her. No, the face of night
Was coldly scornful, like the face of one
Who neither loves nor hates; who sees and knows,
But cares not: the wide gulphs between the clouds.
That moved in rugged masses o'er the sky,
Were sprinkled thick with stars that stared on her
Lifelessly, pitilessly clear and cold;
And deep beneath, the rolling river sped
Under the arches, past the gloomy piles,
Toward the sullen weir, cruel and strong,
Bright-black like liquid steel, and its low sound
Seemed to her morbid ear the utterance
Of a disdainful fate, that, passing on,

All careless yet relentless called to her,
'Come, for the time is come, and thou canst die.'
   Then on a sudden shrieking, 'I can die:
I have lost him and my soul, for he is dead,
And I shall never never see him more;
But I can die—' she raised her arms and ran
Down the dim path, and came upon the weir.
Then had she surely cast her life away,
Upon the seething hissing shroud that spread
Over that grave of waters—but again
Upon her ear, imperiously sweet,
Pathetic, more than human out of Heaven,
And yet with all the nearness of the world,
Fell the child's cry, *his* utterance, '*Kate, O Kate,
I love you—love you!*'
                      And beside the shore
She stayed her steps, and turned, and swooned, and
   fell,
And lay all night 'twixt swoon and sleep: and there
Her father, a despairing broken man,
Aged in a night, found her at early dawn.

    *   *   *   *   *   *

That summer died: and soon the year was dead:
And round the Rectory Farm, from out the snows

That like a mantle of atonement lay
Over the penitent earth, a fair new year
Rose with the crocus; then the violet
Smiled here and there: a sign, a touch of heaven
In lowly earthly places—like a hope
Lovely in meekness, yet so purely strong
It made the live air fragrant all around.
Then one and one, like stars at early night
In the wide heav'n, o'er the wide earth the flowers
Glimmered and beamed and broadened into bloom;
And the year grew beneath the light and warmth
And benison of summer. Summer came,
And on its earliest loveliest day there stood,
Within God's Acre by the ancient church,
Nigh all the hamlet. 'Twas a funeral day:
But spring and summer, joining hand in hand,
Sang, shone, about us and the open grave—
And there we laid 'Deare Childe.'
      And round the grave
We sang that 'JESUS lives,' and from His Love
Henceforth 'nor life, nor death, nor powers of hell,
Can tear us ever.'
     And of those who sang
Were two: a man, on whom might all men see

Written in reverent peace the fear of God—
In peace, yet as it had been taught by pain.
And at his side, and close as love to him,
A beautiful sad woman : sad the face,
For it was grave and set beyond her years,
And 'as by fire' was writ upon its calm,
But sweet and steadfast was the calm ; and Hope
Through all its sacred sadness smiled and sang.

    And my heart sang too, though it wept the while.

Poems on Pictures.

Death as a Friend.

ON THE PICTURE 'DER TOD ALS FREUND.'

PICTURES have voices that the soul can hear
As upon form and feature looks the mind:
Yet are they heard too seldom; for as sound
To the outward sense moves slowly after light,
So, and how often (for we rather love
To look than listen), ere the soul can hear
The mind's eye sees and passes on in haste,
Self-satisfied, unwilling to await
The sweet slow sound. And great the loss: for Art
In such discourse fulfils her perfect work.

'Death as a Friend:' how good and sweet the truth
Here taught so quaintly! Many a time for me,
As it may chance that my inconstant eyes
Forego their wonted haste and heedfully
Linger upon it till my soul can hear,
This picture, like a prophet, on my wall

Takes up its parable. As soft as dew,
Gentle as summer rain on fainting fields,
The sound descends, to quicken, not by fear,
But by refreshment. Many a time when faith,
Tired of her toilsome pilgrim-path too soon,
Was drooping in me, has the voice come down
Persuading her to vigorous life again
And patience, not by terrors of the Lord,
But by the calm constraint of love, Christ's love,
Seen in the dead face of a Christian man.

   The gracious influence is upon me now
In sight and sound. Look with me on the scene
With eyes that see; and who hath ears to hear
Then let him hear.
                It is the heavenly hour
Of earthly life; the one pathetic hour
I' the day of this hard world: when Passion dies,
And Faith and Hope and Charity rule all;
When Peace is nearest, when the light that glows
Is deepest and most tender: when the airs
Breathe Heaven in sighs of joy, as if they blew
Across the border land of Paradise
Into the wild: when there is all the rest
Without the gloom of night, and all the calm

Without the silence and the weight of sleep :—
The sunset hour.
                    Far o'er the landscape looks
A belfry chamber high within the spire
Of some antique cathedral : wide and low
The window, a broad arch of stone unbarred,
Unshaded, opens full upon the west :
And there, beyond the gathered homes of men,
Beyond the fields, the woodland, and the streams,
And last, a long low line of distant hills,
The summer sun is setting. The great orb
Half sunk, half seen, at the far limit glows,
Like the arched summit of a heavenly gate
Opened for some new soul, and for his sake
Flooding with radiance all the outer world
Wherein had passed erewhile his pilgrim days.
  But seems the tender glory most to fall
Over the great cathedral, and there most
Within that belfry chamber, and most there
On one who by the window seems asleep.
The minster's sacristan : and in his home
In that old room, where half his fourscore years
Have known him night and day.
                         Upon the board

Set, like an Altar, 'neath the Holy Sign
Which overhangs it from the grey stone wall,
Remain, in cup and platter placed aside,
The fragments of a simple meal: his chair,
Huge, of rude oak, but darkly bright with age,
Wherein the old man sits as if in sleep,
So near the board the Holy Book thereon
Lies at his hand and open. But his hands,
Together laid and pointed as for prayer
Upon his knees, are still: and still his form,
Stiller than slumber, for no pulse of breath
Heaves the rough robe upon his breast or stirs
The white growth on his lip; the reverend face,
Still also as a monument of stone,
Nor sees nor feels the flood of roseate light
That hides its pallor, shedding o'er the place,
That ancient chamber! hues of love and life
As if it were a bridegroom's on the day
Of his rejoicing!

     True indeed the word!
This is the day that old man weds with joy,
With joy and beauty and eternal youth:
This eve is morn to him of that fair day,
That new fair day begun in Paradise,

Not doomed to die! for there what God had joined
No time shall put asunder.
                            He is dead
To man, he lives to God. Asleep indeed,
Fallen on sleep from poverty and toil
To wake in crowned repose.
                            But came there none
To bid him rise—Angel of Peace to him
Bringing good tidings, saying, 'Enter in
Thou good and faithful'?
                            See, another form
In the old belfry chamber stands erect
Hard by. One rope is grasped within its hand,
And overhead the mighty Tenor tolls,
Obedient, tolls: Oh hear it! solemn-sweet,
How awfully yet tenderly it tolls!
It deepens all the peace it breaks upon
So tolling.
            Listen still! for other sound
Fills every pause: a singer of the woods
Has left the woods for earliest evensong;
There on the window parapet she sings:
Oh never nightingale beneath the moon
So sang as she is singing in this glow

Of love and life! before a dead man's face
And Death.

    For he is Death who standeth there.
The head is bent with reverence, for he stands
On holy ground: but, by the withered hand
That tolls, and by the ghastly face and form
Scarce shrouded by the hooded serge, 'tis Death.
 'O king of terrors, is it thou?'
         '"Tis I :—
But not the king of terrors, the abhorred,
The minister of ill. This am I not,
Not thus I come, to such as him thou seest
Beloved of God: and if thou namest me,
This am I, Death the Friend.'
       'O Death, O friend,
Grant me such grace that when thou callest me
It shall be thus, in peace!'
       'Thou may'st not choose,
Nor is it mine to give, for I am sent:
This be content to know—if thou art His,
Thy summons shall be surely unto peace
If not in peace. Ever to each true soul
Patient in love, the end shall be the same
Though be the calling not as this. To some

It comes abruptly, like a trumpet blast
Pealing at midnight when the streets are still:
To some as out of seeming wasted toil
And purpose unfulfilled, like that which called
Up Nebo's height the prophet from the tribes:
Or there it comes to close a long hard strife,
The war with will and pride, a still small voice
After the wind, the earthquake, and the fire:
Or there to end the body's agonies,
The pangs of want, or torture, or disease,
An "It is finished" whispered down from Heaven
In pain's supreme remission. But not thus
It came to him before thee, but in peace
As unto peace. Behold, his eyes are closed;
I called his spirit, and it passed, in sleep;
And brighter angels—for I cannot rise
In that pure air—bore it to final rest,
To larger knowledge of the Lord he loved,
And gladder service.'
       Such, the while I gaze,
The seeming utterance in my spirit's ear
Of Death the Friend. Still listen, O my soul!
Out of the calm as of the happier land,
'Mid hues of glory daylight never knows,

In reverend presence of the saint asleep,
Still hear descending out of the unseen
The sweet deep tolling; hear the rapt bird sing
The evensong of life; hear Death the Friend
Utter his oracle of peace assured
To those who love and wait. Then go thy way
Waiting in love till he is sent to thee.

Tired.

ON A PICTURE OF A TIRED CHILD.

ONLY the noon of day:
    And yet, tired out with too long play
The little hands sink slowly down,
The little face is weary grown,
As if the sun had set and slipped away,—
    And yet 'tis noon of day.

    How blithe she was this morn:
With such a smile of merry scorn,
As gaily from her sunny brow
She swept the truant hair—and now
So wearily, so wistfully, forlorn:
    Blithe as she was this morn!

    As one whom vague surprise
Has seized unwittingly, she lies;
And looks out on the world of change,
So drear and dim, so still and strange,

With wordless questions in her wide blue eyes,
    Lost in a vague surprise.

    Where are those morning joys,
Those dear delights of games and toys?
The toys survive, the joys are dead,
The form remains, but life has fled:
Why should dull silence drown your happy noise,
    Ye merry morning joys?

    So tired—yet sleep delays:
No spell has curtained yet her gaze:
'Tis more than weary limb reveals
That aspect grave. The spirit feels
A mystic shadow stealing o'er her days;
    And sleep the while delays.

    O child Ecclesiast,
Who know'st the pain of pleasures past!
Unconscious questioner! thine eyes
Ask, 'Is there nought that satisfies?
Has earth no joy that will for ever last?'
    Thou true Ecclesiast!

    Ah, soon for thee the shade
Shall vanish, when thy head is laid

Sweetly upon thy mother's breast,
And eyes shall close, and heart shall rest:
There lying down thou shalt not be afraid!
So passing through the shade.

Perchance, too, in thy sleep—
That short sweet death, so still and deep—
An answer shalt thou find in dreams
Of fields and flowers, and woods and streams,
Where one good Shepherd folds His happy sheep;
So blest shall be thy sleep.

Tired too, there are who know,
Alas, more consciously than thou,
This emptiness of emptinesses,
The world's delights, the world's caresses,
Those morning pleasures that so quickly go—
This wearily they know.

And they, like thee, ere long,
Shall fall on sleep, where grief and wrong
Shall vex no more; and, as they rest,
Childlike upon their Father's breast,
Shall hear not this world's plaint, but that world's
song;
So shall it be ere long!

Saint Augustine and Monica.

ON THE PICTURE BY ARY SCHEFFER.

'Colloquebamur ergò valdè dulciter, et præterita obliviscentes in ea quæ ante sunt extenti quærebamus inter nos apud præsentem veritatem quod Tu es, qualis futura esset vita æterna sanctorum, quam nec oculus vidit, nec auris audivit, nec in cor hominis ascendit.'— S. Augustini Confess.: Lib. ix. cap. 10.

'Now they desire a better country, that is, an heavenly.'— Hebrews xi. 16.

THE son of many tears and many prayers,
 And she, the mother who had wept and prayed,
Sit side by side, and with expectant eyes
Look for the coming of the day of God.

O Picture, worthy of a saint in art!
O painted Poem! eloquent of truth
Which our vain hearts are slow to learn and love,
That here is not our rest, that never here
Find we our home—here, where our summers die:
Summers of pleasure, all too fiercely bright,
Summers of our ambition, vexed with storms,
Scarcely enjoyed, albeit so wildly sought,

And then soon ended—here, where winter comes
Cheered with no promise of a future spring:
Winter of buried joys and dead desires,
Winter of failing hand and feeble brain,
Winter so cold with frozen streams of hope,
Winter, so dark with growing clouds of pain,
Winter that comes and stays till all is night.

This is the truth writ sternly in his face—
A face sharp-lined and hollowed as by fire,
The former burning of a passionate heart
Which spent so long its fruitless force on sin,
Seeking but finding not perfection here.
Yet more we read than this! O steadfast eyes,
Lifted in gaze that reaches past the world:
O calm still mien of confidence and strength,
O features settled in sublime repose,
O clasping hand that speaks communion here
In perfect peace, foretaste of perfect joy:
How is your silence eloquent with sound,
Soul-piercing, even as the trumpet tones
Of that great angel bearing thro' mid Heav'n
The everlasting gospel!
     As I gaze

The world fades off, and all my meaner self,
Abashed as in a presence all too strong
To be withstood, too holy to be scorned,
Shrinks from me for a season; and my soul,
Its new life freed awhile of that dull weight,
The 'body of this death,' finds wings to rise
More near to God and heav'n—finds clearer ken
For those deep things, except by faith, unseen,
Finds hearing ears for blessed harmonies
Which mix not with the echoes of our life
Its music or its laughter.—Far away
Their vision reaches onward, and with theirs
Mine also, and I catch the same glad sounds,
Voices that herald in a coming joy,
Which fall upon their ears, and in their lips
Beget alternate utterance.
      Thus he speaks:
'Lo, in the stormy west the day lies dead—
The bleak drear day—the sun which was its life
Is hid in boundless depth behind the hills,
And keeps its orient for a fairer morn.
E'en so has died my wild day of this world,
And so my life is hid with Christ in God,
So waiteth on, till He, my life shall come,

And give His glory as he gave His life,
According to His word.   I wait for Him.'

   She taketh up his speech :
                      'I wait for Him,
E'en as I waited for His grace to thee :
In strength of trust I waited till it came.
I served Him day and night with tears and prayers,
Yea many heavy days and weary nights,
And yet no sign, and still I prayed and wept ;
Then the great gift came brooding o'er the deep
Of thy dark soul, and then the voice of power
Commanding light to break across the gloom,
Then the full day ! He hath fulfilled His word
For me in thee,—He will for all His saints ;
And so, in strength of trust I wait for Him.'

   'Glory to Him !' he saith, 'I wait for Him ;
I, who was alien in the sinful past
But now am near, would fain be nearer still,—
Nearer for love and service—and that past
I cast behind me, stretching forth my hands
Unto that future, when mine eyes shall see
The Master face to face, when I shall know

E'en as I am known. How will come that hour!
With what great visions such as man's dim eye
Hath never seen: with sounds that his dull ear
Hath never heard, with unimagined bliss
Flooding the soul with joys that cannot die;
With what sweet peace, closing the strife of sin,
The war of Time! O Lord, I wait for Thee!'

' Yea, though 'tis peace,' she answers, ' for mine eyes
Have seen His great salvation, I would go,
As from the twilight to the perfect day,
From peace to fuller peace. Oh come, sweet hour,
Bright with the golden promise! come and bring
All heavenly harmonies unheard before,
All sights unseen: Oh, come, with all things new!
Sin ended, sorrow closed, His reign begun!
O Master, Prince of Peace, I wait for Thee!'

And now, as though it may no longer be
That they, made one for evermore in Him,
Should have divided utterance, in accord,
While with hands closer clasped they sit and gaze
With quiet faithful eyes more keenly fixed
As if with nearer vision of that day,
Rises from twain one voice,

'We wait for Thee,
Oh long-expected, long-desired, for Thee!
Hast Thou not said, and shalt Thou not make good?
" Quick is My coming!" therefore all our cry
Is his to whom Thou gavest of Thine hour
Apocalyptic vision : "Even so,
Lord Jesus, come;" roll back Thy heavens and come,
O Saviour, unto Whom are all things given,
Come with Thy voice of love and claim Thine own!
Good Shepherd,—knowing all and known of all,—
O come, and call Thy sheep from off the wild!
Monarch, in mercy and in power supreme,
Take for Thine own the kingdoms of the world!
God! Whose high thoughts and ways are over ours,
As yonder heaven sublime above the earth,
Come in Thine own good time : we wait for Thee!'

Setting Sail.

ON A PICTURE OF THREE CHILDREN ON THE SHORE.

THE Spring-tide air was breathing balm
   Upon the waters all the night,
And scarce they moved when morning calm
   Gave waking soft to slumber light,
And down the shore came children three
To launch a mimic argosy.

Said one—he was a noble boy,
   And at their gallant mock emprise
Looked keenly, with the glittering joy
   Of dawning purpose in his eyes—
"Thus will I sail from strand to strand,
And fight for God and fatherland!"

Said one she was the elder child,
   And older yet in all her ways,
She was so motherly and mild,
   So meekly wise beyond her days

'O'er sea or land I'll never roam,
While father wants his maid at home.'

Then lisped a third—in whose sweet face
   Awoke a wistful dreamy smile,
Reflection of the loving grace
   Of one whom she had lost awhile—
'I'll sail away from year to year,
Until I find my mother dear.'

    .   .   .   .   .

Full fifty years brought evenfall
   Upon that morning of their life,
And, scarred with wounds, a seaman tall
   Came slowly homeward from the strife;
Long had he served from strand to strand
The cause of God and fatherland.

He found a man of ninety years,
   Whose dying eyes were turned to bless
A maiden old, whose gentle tears
   Fell quicker at that mute caress:
In death that loving hand and eye
For him, as ever, still were nigh.

The third? She sailed, ah! long ago,
   And found her mother dear at rest:
And where? It is enough to know
   'Twas in an Eden of the blest—
'Twas far away, beyond the foam,
She found her mother dear at home.

Christus Consolator.

ON THE PICTURE BY ARY SCHEFFER, ILLUSTRATIVE OF THE SAVIOUR'S INVITATION, 'COME UNTO ME, ALL YE THAT LABOUR AND ARE HEAVY-LADEN, AND I WILL GIVE YOU REST.'

ONE over all supreme, the King of kings,
    The 'very God,' behold Him throned on cloud;
Yet now not such as no man hath beheld,
Or can behold; not unapproachable—
Upon whose face no man can look and live—
Not dreadful with the ensigns of such power,
Darkness of rolling thunders rent with flame,
The voice exceeding loud, the quivering rocks,
As on that day, in utterance of the law,
Kept far away from Sinai's awful mount
The quaking tribes; not now the terrible Judge,
Before whose just wrath cowers a guilty world;
Not such behold Him!—but the Prince of Peace,

Giving the bounty of His great goodwill,
Not as the world gives to the rich and strong,
But to the poor and weak: the Lord of Love,
Who standeth not apart, nor passeth by
Saying, 'Be warmed and filled,' to those that need,
But sitteth in their midst, with gracious hands
Outstretched for instant aid—a present help
For every trouble; yea, the 'very Man,'
Acquaint with pain by His own suffering,
Inviting men by His humanity,
Saying, 'Come unto ME, ye weary ones!
I will refresh you; I will give you rest,
Ye heavy-laden.'

     Round about His form
They gather, gazing on Him. In His face,
Oh what pathetic meanings! eloquent
Of far-off days of suffering and of toil,
Far-off, but unforgotten; yet not less
Of present calm, in consciousness of power,
The peace of God, that cannot fail or fear;
A calm that breathes compassion, in its strength
Divine, but in its pain-taught tenderness
Most human—yea, a calm that tells of rest
Won for the weary in most weary hours

Of earthly woe; deep, like an infinite sea
Of tears, formed when the fountains of all pain
Were broken up, and gathered in one flood,
Then smoothed and stilled to this serene repose,
A calm that none may vex for evermore,
Whereto all hearts may come: a calm of love,
Infinite love, breadth, length, and depth, and height,
Omnipotent, yet passionless, so full
Of radiance that it makes eternal noon,
Fairer than all the suns of all the worlds,
Yet such that meekest eyes may gaze thereon
Undrooping.   So they gaze who round His form
Are gathered—gaze upon the face of GOD
Unsmitten, for it is the face of Him
Who was the MAN of sorrows.   Sorrowful
They came, and in that presence straightway fell
The long life-burden; in that light of love
The old perplexing shadows fled away,
And from their souls a song goes up to greet
The spiritual morning; in that calm
Dies all the tumult of the strife with sin—
The voices of unrest and of despair
Are hushed for ever.

                        Young and old are there,
The matron and the maiden side by side,
The young man and the sage of many years,
The unlearned and the wise.
                        And unto all
Flows the same utterance—serene with power.
And soft with love, and deep with tenderness—
Saying, 'Come unto ME, ye weary souls!
I will refresh you; I will give you rest,
Ye heavy-laden.'
                        Kneeling at His side,
With her wan face low bowed upon His arm,
Behold a form thick-shrouded from the gaze
Of a most scornful world, which hath despoiled,
Then marked her outcast with the brand of shame;
And she is closest there of all the throng.
How shall so great a sinner come so near?
May lips so guilty touch that sacred robe,
And not defile? Oh, not the less to her
Because she was a sinner more than all,
But most to her whose need was more than all,
Was access given, invitation said,
'Come unto ME!' and she hath heard the words,
The wonderful sweet words, with hungry ears,

And on the dry waste of her penitent soul
'Thy sins are all forgiven' hath fall'n like rain
On thirsty lands. To whom is much forgiven,
Loveth the more, and her exceeding love
Hath drawn her nearest.
     See, the outstretched Arm
O'er which she bows her low adoring head
For yet another captive of despair
Worketh deliverance. Waken as from death,
Thou prisoner of sin! for lo! thy chains,
Touched by that pitiful, resistless Hand,
Slip from thee. Open to the glorious light
Thy long-closed eyes, whereon the dungeon gloom
May weigh no more; and greet, for it is thine,
The liberty wherewith He maketh free
The tied and bound, who out of prison depths
To Him lift up their cry.
     One kneeleth there
Upon whose face the tale of many years,
Deep written, tells of sad humanity—
Of the life mortal with its pains and cares.
Like channels left upon the barren side
Of some grey mountain where on days of storm
The ancient torrents held their way, so here,

Plain are the hollowed traces of past tears;
But as upon the scathed and furrowed rock,
When winter lies asleep, and winds are still,
The benediction of the morning throws
Its most pathetic beauty—more sublime
In beauty for the solemn evidence
Of sternest visitation—so, behold,
Upon this worn face, gazing at the Christ—
For souls the orient light of heavenly day—
The marks of woe that mar it for the world
Take rare and reverend beauty in the glow
Of the eternal brightness. Evermore
That heart, world-weary, shall be satisfied
In peace, the dim eyes glad, for on them shines
His Face of light, whose Voice of love declares,
'I give thee rest.'

      Ah! fair and young in years,
But old with one great sorrow, she who kneels
Hard by: the sapling by the aged pine,
Both scathed, but that one by a hundred storms,
This by a single stroke, with grievous power,
To do the work of a tempestuous age
As in a moment. Suddenly her life,
So full of present pleasure and glad hope,

Seemed far away, unreal and remote
As some evanished dream of long ago.
The world seemed strange, so dark it was and drear,
And alien voices filled it, harsh and hard,
And all experience seemed a bounded land
Between two graves—the grave of that lost dream,
And that for which she long'd of this changed life.
O broken heart! there is but One may bring
Balm for thy pain; but lo! He passeth by:
'Arise!' He calleth, 'I will give thee rest;
Come unto ME.' And she arose and came;
And now she gazes ever in His face,
Her great Physician, who hath poured the balm
Of precious healing in the grievous wound;
And evermore her life shall glide away,
Like some still stream at holy eventide,
To find, when He shall will, more perfect peace,
In heaven's eternal sea.
      A mother there
Lays down her silent burden at His feet—
Her little one, her lost one, her beloved,
The darling of a life so bare of joys;
How can she lose it? Oh, it is not lost.
She comes and lays it there, and He, she knows—

The great good Shepherd of the heavenly fold—
Will stoop and take it up within His arms,
And keep it there from all that might befall,
Safe—safe for ever. Let His will be done,
Whose perfect knowledge works with perfect love,
And orders well. 'It *is* well with the child'
Amidst her tears she murmurs, at the feet
Of Him Who wept for Lazarus, till they said,
'Lo, how He loved him!' Who will comfort her,
Despising not her tears, because of love.

As some tired pilgrim from the pitiless glare
Beneath 'a great rock in a weary land'
Finds shelter and repose, a Poet sits
Low at the Saviour's side. The leaves of bay
(As though to her apostle nature gave,
Like Pentecostal gift, her sylvan tongues)
Meet o'er his brow. But lowly sits he there;
O'er the crossed arms inclines the reverent head,
And from the grave still face the deep-set eyes
Look in as on the tablets of a heart
Whereon the story of a faultful past
Is writ in many sorrows, read with pain.
Oh, bitter-sweet has been the world's applause!
For Fame, whom far away he saw so fair,

So passing fair, crown'd with immortal light,
And girt with rolling music out of heaven,
When he drew near to claim her, slipp'd away,
And yet away; and when at length she stood
And crown'd him, lo! the glory round her form
Grew pale and earthly, and the heavenly swell
Of that high music took a lower tone,
And died ere long, or else it seemed to die.
Then in a scornful mood, 'In mine own soul,
Ever,' he said, 'henceforth my quest is made;
There will I find the comfort that remains,
The peace that fills, the joy that satisfies.'
Then he did rise and dwell apart from men;
But not alone: voices of other souls
Spoke from the silent pages in his ears
Of truth and beauty, and he sought and found,
In all fair arts and deep philosophies,
Food for his meditations and his dreams.
But most with Nature he was wont to take
Sweet converse as of old, who, loving him,
Spread out before him all the mysteries
She veils from common eyes. But, ah! not yet
The end was found, the comfort that remain'd,
The peace that fill'd, the joy that satisfied;

For there was that which vex'd him day by day:
Sometimes a quick wild cry that smote like fear,
Sometimes from far a hollow voice of scorn,
Sometimes a sigh within him like the moan
Of some lost sea that rolls without a shore,
But ever with one burden, 'It is vain!
Thou hast not found; doubtless thou shalt not find.'
Then, lo! when now his soul was sad indeed
And humble, dawn'd on him with growing light
This vision of The Christ—a Form of power,
A Face of love, his dreams had never known;
And, crowning all the vague desire of years,
Which arts, and nature, and philosophies,
The lore of every age and all the world,
Had left unanswered, fell upon his heart,
That voice of the God-Man, 'Come unto me,
And I will give thee comfort that remains,
And peace that fills, and joy that satisfies.'

And now, behold, he sits beneath his Lord
As one whose quest is over: unto whom
The end has come like calm at eventide
After the restless day; a humble soul,
Mindful of all its past, but by that love,

Despite the past, fulfilled with present peace,
And some sure hope of bliss that is to be.

  O Christ! O Rest of heaven! O Peace of God!
O Life of souls! O Light in sorrow's depth!
O Hope in sin's despair! Thou only Strength
That ever overcomes, Thou only Joy
That cannot droop or die, Thou only Love
That faileth not! O Jesus, God and Man,
Be ours as theirs, to pardon, to set free,
To pity, to console, to satisfy,
To crown with love for ever and for ever!

The Cradle on the Shore.

ON THE PICTURE BY EUGENE WEST.

WITH scarce a murmur, scarce a ripple's motion,
    E'en where his tidal waters shoreward creep,
Careless of coming tempests, Father Ocean
    Lies in the glowing sunshine fast asleep.

Like some great giant of our childhood's stories,
    Charm'd by the glamour of a fairy queen,
Beneath this overflow of noonday glories
    We see no more the fury which has been.

The children's feet fall trustfully upon him,
    And by the soft swell of his dreamy tide
It seems as if the sleeper felt them on him,
    And in a fond contentment moved and sigh'd.

In the cliff cottage lies their tiny sister—
    Not safer she than they from every harm,
Where haply half an hour ago they kiss'd her,
    Leaping and smiling on their mother's arm.

See, they have brought her cradle to his waters,
    To cleanse it in a bath of odours there—
Dearest and best to all his sons and daughters—
    The fresh salt fragrance of the wave and air.

Child of the ocean, like a fond caressing,
    Let the sweet odour compass thee around,
Like an unspoken and an unseen blessing,
    Like wordless song and music without sound:

Type of a holier influence hovering o'er thee
    From the far ocean of a fuller Grace,
E'en as this noon reflects the brighter glory
    Of the deep heaven beyond this azure space.

A Boy's Reverie

OVER AN OLD PICTURE.

WHAT shall I be?
    I'd like to be a soldier, strong and tall,
Like Grandpapa, drawn in the picture here;
And be the first to hear the trumpet's call,
And be the first to scale the castle wall.
    But then, you see,
The worst of it is this, Mamma, poor dear—
Just because these brave fighters sometimes fall,—
Won't hear about this soldiering at all!
    Papa's a clergyman,
And nobody's one-half as good as he,
Nor ever was, *I* think, since time began;
No, and I don't believe will ever be:
    I know Mamma thinks so;
And that's the reason partly, I dare say,
She hopes with all her heart her boy some day
Will lead good people in his father's way.

And when I tell her 'No,
I want to be a soldier of the Queen,'
She says (and dear old Auntie just the same)
'That there's a soldier's service nobler far,
With surer triumph and a grander fame,
Than any fighting in an earthly war;
Great battles that no eye has ever seen
'Gainst foes more fierce than ever men have been;
And that a clergyman *does* wear a sword
As captain in the armies of the Lord.'

I think I know what she and Auntie mean,
And like to hear them tell of it; but still
I should so like a sword that I can *see*,
Like Grandpapa's, and wield it in my hand,
Just as he's painted here upon the hill,
While all the soldiers charge at his command;
That's just how I should like to look, so grand!

Oh, dear, oh, dear, I don't know what to do!
I shouldn't worry, if I only knew;
But now it's quite a burden on my mind,
Because in both directions I'm inclined.
I'd like to be a good man, like Papa,

And, best of all, it would so please Mamma,
But then, I want to fight like Grandpapa.
 I'm in a regular fix:
Nurse says that I must wait, I'm only six,
And this time ten years will be time enough
To make a fuss about what I shall be.
I don't care what *she* says, because, you see,
Every one knows old women talk such stuff.

 There! I declare she's calling me again.
The cross old thing!—hark at her overhead:
'Come, Master Johnnie, time you were asleep!'
 One thing is very plain,
When I'm a man (oh, how the time does creep!
I wish it could be done as soon as said!)
Unless I choose, I'll *never* go to bed!

The Soliloquy of a Rationalistic Chicken.

ON THE PICTURE OF A NEWLY HATCHED CHICKEN CON-
TEMPLATING THE FRAGMENTS OF ITS NATIVE SHELL.

MOST strange!
Most queer,—although most excellent a change!
Shades of the prison-house, ye disappear!
My fettered thoughts have won a wider range,
    And, like my legs, are free;
No longer huddled up so pitiably:
Free now to pry and probe, and peep and peer,
    And make these mysteries out.
Shall a free-thinking chicken live in doubt?
For now in doubt undoubtedly I am:
    This problem's very heavy on my mind,
And I'm not one to either shirk or sham:
    I won't be blinded, and I won't be blind!

Now, let me see;
First, I would know how did I get in *there?*
Then, where was I of yore?
Besides, why didn't I get out before?

Bless me!
Here are three puzzles (out of plenty more)
Enough to give me pip upon the brain.!
But let me think again.
How do I know I ever *was* inside?
Now I reflect, it is, I do maintain,
Less than my reason, and beneath my pride
To think that I could dwell
In such a paltry miserable cell
As that old shell.
Of course I couldn't! How could *I* have lain,
Body and beak and feathers, legs and wings,
And my deep heart's sublime imaginings,
In there?

I meet the notion with profound disdain;
It's quite incredible; since I declare
(And I'm a chicken that you can't deceive)
What I can't understand I won't believe.

Where *did* I come from, then? Ah! where, indeed?
This is a riddle monstrous hard to read.
    I have it! Why, of course,
All things are moulded by some plastic force
Out of some atoms somewhere up in space,
Fortuitously concurrent anyhow :—
    There, now!
That's plain as is the beak upon my face.

    What's that I hear?
My mother cackling at me! Just her way,
So prejudiced and ignorant *I* say;
So far behind the wisdom of the day!

    What's old I *can't* revere.
Hark at her. 'You're a little fool, my dear,
    That's quite as plain, alack!
As is the piece of shell upon your back!'
How bigoted! upon my back, indeed!
    I don't believe it's there:
For I can't *see* it; and I do declare,
    For all her fond deceivin',
What I can't see I never will believe in!

Country-Born.

ON A PICTURE OF A FARM-YARD.

OH me—my country-life that's gone!
    The fields, the woods, the flowers,
The dear old farm, the lane of limes
    We ran to in the showers,
And each belovèd nook that knew
    Those old delicious hours:—
To dream of these and wake up here,
Makes the drear town grow doubly drear.

There's not a place that I forget,
    Nor thing I cannot see:
At morning Dobbin's in his stall,
    Just as he used to be:
At evening Nancy in the yard
    Still feeds the brood with me:
Mother at night when I'm abed
Comes back to kiss me from the dead.

I see the nook where father sat,
   With mother near his side :
I see the room above the porch,
   Where little Alice died—
Ah, she went first, but nothing now
   Can her and them divide :
Their names, all three, are on one stone,
And only I am left alone.

How doleful is this town to me !
   The sun shines all in vain :
With all his beams he'll never make
   The street a linden lane :
I often think I'd rather see,
   Instead, the sighing rain
Fall, like innumerable tears,
In sorrow for those happy years !

A Sea-side Reverie.

ON THE PICTURE OF A STILL SEA.

CALM sea:
  One water broad and bright beneath the sun,
Near and afar, in peace and silence, one;
The long shore-shallow with the distant deep,
  One still immensity:
    Infinitude fallen on sleep.

How bright and beautiful a peace!
One fain would listen for the sleeper's breath—
The giant sleeper, sleeping like a child
By some sweet mother into rest beguiled—
For this is calm of slumber, not of death;
The mighty pulses only seem to cease;
  The great heart of the sea,
  Throbbing unheard, invisibly,
Beats not the less with the resistless power
Of his fierce anger's most tremendous hour.

His passions only hide—how soon,
And whence we know not, there may come
A cloud across the splendid noon,
And winds to wake him from this summer swoon;
And then, no longer dumb,
Shall his loud tongue tell fearfully and far
Again the giant girds himself for war!

Yet, though this quiet marks no dearth
Of strength and life—repose but not decay—
Here lurketh Death; O great, and strong, and free,
Death waits to lay his palsying hand on thee!
Is it not writ that, on a day
When sweeter heavens shall smile on purer earth,
There shall be no more sea?
Yea, thou shalt die:
What matter if thine hour be far or nigh?
Lo, not less surely ebbs thy life away
Than yonder splendour fails from off the land,
Or thine own dreamy tide is slipping from the strand!

Calm Sea:
Repose how rare, and, as the moments fleet,
Ever to seem more wonderful and sweet!

The little children do not shrink
To trust their tender steps beyond his brink,
So faint a ripple rolls he to their feet,
    Only a kiss it seems
Of one who loves them in the land of dreams.
Sunny and placid are their childish years:
Pure pleasure's light, not passion's, in their eyes,
Calm on the wide depths of their sleeping souls,
They reck not of such possibilities
As lie, within my vision, there,
And make my heart already sick with fears,
    Because already in mine ears
    The wind grows wild, the storm-wave rolls,
And cries go up in pain, and vows in prayer,
Mid silences, more dreadful, of despair.

    Uncertain Sea, uncertain Life,
Of both how fair the calm, how quick the strife!
    Yet, this side heaven, shall both be dear:
The 'Sea is His' whose are yon depths above,
And Life is His whose gifts are all of love.
    Away! thou poor pale Fear,
O Sea, O Life, for storm or calm we stand
'Neath the safe keeping of our Father's hand.

Yet if, O Sea, thou art so dear,
So dear as this, we cannot spare thee here,
Shall we not miss thee in the glorious Land?—
   Nay, for thou pleasest eye and ear,
Sole image of that longed-for Infinite:
      O image faint and far!
   So love we as our all of light—
While *here* we sojourn—day's majestic star,
There never to be seen, too dimly bright,
Nor missed where, born of God, those jasper glories
      are.

   O Life, despite thine ills, so fair,
Is this unworthy that we love thee *here?*
O nay, because we hold thee dear
   More gladly will we let thee go,
For love of thee makes longing to be *there*,
      Beyond thy bounds above,
Where in immortal fulness we shall know
   The grandeur and the beauty and the love,
Whereof we had by thee faint foretaste here below.

      O Sea, O Life,
The pilgrim lingers where he may not dwell,

Lingers with hopeful heart and loving eyes,
    And with a voice of praise
For such a grace shed on the weary ways
    That lie between him and the skies;
Such grace of calm or grandeur as can tell
Prophetic stories of that far-off home
Whereto at last his happy feet shall come.
    So, till his pilgrimage is o'er,
And till his steps shall cease upon the shore,
No craven fears his loyal faith shall quell:
In peace or passion, in repose or strife,
He loves thee well, O Sea, O Life, he loves thee well!

Miscellaneous Poems.

The Sea of Galilee.

> 'Though inland far we be,
> Our souls have sight of that immortal Sea.'
> WORDSWORTH'S *Ode*.

THERE is a river in the Holiest Land
    Beyond the evil world, whose streams make glad
The spiritual city; overswept
By the still breathing of one equal wind
From the celestial hills, the crystal waves
For ever flowing, yet for ever calm,
Made music in their course, the undersong
Of that great strain of Moses and the Lamb
The angels longed for once, and love to hear
From saints who sing upon the jasper sea.
    There is a river in a holy land
Yet in the evil world, whose streams make glad
The hearts of pilgrims journeying far away
On to that Golden City: memories
Of many forms and voices, and of One,

The 'chief among ten thousand,' over it
Breathe like a mystic wind: its lowly waves,
Less lovely to the vision of the world
Than Abana and Pharpar, are to these
More beautiful than all the brighter floods
Of fairer lands: and all of sound and scene
They furnish of delight for ever find
Centre and fulness in one silver sea.

A still small Sea. No majesty of earth
Makes its renown: no boundless multitude
Of league-long waters roll from land to land,
From winter unto summer shores: no wealth
Or might of argosy or armament
Rides or reposes on its breast. By day,
Save when in wrath the sudden winds descend,
Or wild birds cry above the darkening shoals,
Sits Silence there, imperial gentleness
Upon an argent throne: and reigns by night,
All the celestial jewels on her robe,
None vexing her dominion, save perchance
Some solitary fisher,[1] sad at heart,
In cheerless labour wears the hours away.

[1] The heavy prohibitive tax on boats is so ruinous that from A.D. 1738 to 1860, no one has noted more than one boat on the lake. See Macgregor, *On the Jordan*, p. 38.

A still small sea. The mountains gird it in;
There in the orient gathered stern and strong
From northern Bashan unto Gadara,
Like warders, clad in sombre hues, updrawn
In even line: a silent guard of hills
Bareheaded, gaunt: with many a riven rock
Grey or dark red, and many a grassy slope
Flowing in waves of green toward the plain.
There at the sunset keep they watch and ward
In stranger mood, height answering not to height
But broken in array,[1] and mingling far
With Safed's craggy summits and the horns
Of Hattin's[2] holy hill, and where the glow
Streams through the groves of oak and terebinth,
With the long curve of Tabor throwing down
Softly its purple shadow. Still they rise,
Fair terraces, wild gorges, pressing on
In lowlier line, on to the northern throne
Where far away ascends the nearest heaven
Imperial Hermon. Sovereign lord he seems
Amid the kneeling hills; or when the sun
At even crowns his everlasting snows

---

[1] See Stanley, *Sinai and Palestine*, p. 370.
[2] The traditional scene of the Sermon on the Mount.

Like the perpetual altar of their praise
Where overhangs the golden incense-cloud
Of their pure worship. So he stood of old,
When the Incarnate Son in Galilee,
A man of sorrows, was despised of men:
So shall he stand when as the King of kings
The CHRIST returns to reign.

       A still small Sea:
Now like a smile of God amid the frowns
Of treeless hills, but once a lower deep
Of that dark hollow wrought of old by shock
Of fires infernal, from the mountain base
Of Lebanon to Moab.[1] But the dews
That fall on Hermon, and the springs that run
Among the valleys, swelled the river of God
To fill ere long with living waters pure
Death's drear abyss.

      It is the Sea of Life:
Among God's seven seas[2] His sole elect:
Not as that other in the stricken south,
Wherein its river finds mysterious grave,

---

[1] See Stanley, *Sinai and Palestine*, p. 370.
[2] In Lightfoot (i. 6), the following Rabbinical belief is quoted: "I have create! seven seas, saith the Lord, but out of them I have chosen none but the sea of Gennesareth."

The Sea of Death, wherein is naught that lives,
Whereby no blossom blows, or singing bird
Makes happy morning music; but it lies
Gehenna of the seas, and o'er it reigns
Another sadder silence evermore.

  Not such Gennesaret! on its silver strand
Here gently sloping, broken there by rocks,
Whence trail in the sweet wave or woo the air
Green mosses and the tresses of the fern,
Fails not the oleander, night and day,
'The tree the Lord hath planted by the streams,'
Dark-leaved, bright-blossomed. Follows flower on
    flower
And fruit on fruit, these shores along, as snow
Succeeds to snow on Hermon. Sang of old,
What time a thousand fishers thronged the waves,
These toilers to their fellows mid the flocks,
Keeping cold vigil high on Gadara,
Or wandering long through many a parched ravine,
'Come down and drink the freshness of the Nile
And share the wealth of Egypt.' All around
From fair Bataiha's plain, where Jordan finds,
Hard by the lonely palms,[1] a gate of flowers

[1] See Stanley, p. 372.

And darkly speeds him to the pure embrace
Of clearer waters—on to steep Kerak,
Whence he must wind to the sepulchral sea,
Fresh life shows greenly; high in tangled brakes,
In thorn and willow, and in rarer palm,
Low in the drooping ferns and feathery reeds,
And grassy banks that underlie or scale
The bases of the hills.
     But loveliest,
Edged by Bethsaida's fairest fringe of pearl,
And closed by gentler heights, the crescent plain
Of Gennesar[1] the blest! O Naphtali,
Here found thy princes, as in Paradise,
The fulness of Jehovah's grace, at rest
Within His boundless favour!
      'Tis a land
Of halcyon seasons: Beulah of the north:
Here nature's sweet ambition[2] reconciles
Her leafy sons of alien climes; grow here
The northern walnut and the southern palm,
The fig, the olive, and the vine, and all

---

[1] *Gennesar* is the name of the plain given by Josephus (*Bell J.* iii. 10. 8.) The first part of the word is no doubt Gani 'Gardens;' the latter, 'Sar,' is perhaps Prince, referring to the Princes of Naphtali (cf Deut. xxxiii 21)

[2] See Josephus, *B J.* iii. 10. 8

Vie only in a happy strife to crown
Each golden month with fruits. Upon the lawns,
By the soft ripple of melodious rills,
Or by the prouder fountain-flow, that swell
The four bright rivers of this Eden land,
Bloom myriad flowers: the 'lilies of the field,'
More lustrous than the pomp of Solomon,
Smiling above the hollows, or below,
Fire-like amid the shade: so gleams the air,
Cleft by the glancing wings of beauteous birds:
So the sweet gloom of garden and of glen
Is quickened with their song.
                              Yes, fair thou art,
Plain of the chosen Sea—but fairer still
For that in thee awhile did bloom for souls
The Rose of Sharon. On this wave and shore
The divine fragrance of immortal deeds
And words that shall not perish in the wreck
Of earth and heaven, was breathed, and lingers still
As that day draws more near when He shall come,
Who from His waiting children is but gone
A little while away.
                    Stood here,[1] perchance,

---

[1] The opinion of some, that the shore of the Lake was the scene of the incident recorded in St. John i. 36, is at least possible.

Strange presence from the southern wilderness,
Amid this grace and plenty, gaunt and stern,
The last of all the prophets, as he cried,
With reverent gesture at one silent Form,
Tranced into vision of the Precious Blood,
The cry that carries on from age to age,
The evangel everlasting, and for all,
' Behold the Lamb of God !'
                                  His home was here,
And ' His own city ;' for Whom heaven is home,
Whose City is the great Jerusalem,
Clad in God's glory by the hyaline
Eternal Sea.
                Yet, O Capernaum !
Where art thou ? O ' exalted unto heaven !'
That wast the home and city of thy God,
Where art thou ? Phosphor of the cities nine,
The white-robed princes of the silver sea,
How art thou fallen ? Chorazin is no more,
Bethsaida, Magdala, Tiberias,
They are not ; save a few poor walls and towers,
That stare half hidden in their place of doom,
Like ' bones beside the pit ' of death. But thou—
Thou in whose streets the living tide, that flowed

From fair Damascus Zionwards,[1] made one
Gentile and Jew, children of every land—
Thou art not found! Gennesaret knows thee not:
She lies in all her loveliness forlorn,
And has nor voice nor sign from hill to sea
To mark thy tomb and say '"Twas here she reigned,
City of waters.'
    Yet most bright in thee
The 'Great Light' shone which sprang in Nephthalim,
Galilee of the nations,[2] unto souls
Wrapt in the shades of death. Within thy gates,
Or on thy shore, the blind beheld His face
Who is more fair than all the sons of men;
The lame man leaped in praise; the leper's voice
Forgot in happy song his old sad cry;
The sick man's moan of weariness or pain
Was heard no more; this father for a son
At point to die, that for a daughter dead,—
Weeping and praying—heard one word of power,
And ceased to weep, or wept again for joy!
Here, in that Place of Prayer the Roman gave,
The baffled fiend before 'The Holy One'

---

[1] The highway between Damascus and Jerusalem ran through Capernaum.
[2] St. Matthew iv. 14-16.

Fled shrieking. Sons of thine they were who heard
On Hattin's Mount the Blessings that have flowed
Thence to a longing world, and ever flow.
On thine He had compassion in the wild;
Good Shepherd of the homeless sheep. They saw
Within thy walls and courts, or by the wave,
His marvels many and great, and heard the words
Which never man so spake. Wisdom of God,
And Power of God, Light of the World, the CHRIST,
Was manifest to none as unto thee!

    Lost City! memory's phantom by the sea,
How cries thy silence, with a bitter cry,
To yonder waters: 'Go in Jordan's stream,
Utter a dirge in Siddim's awful vale:
Say to the relics there, that are not hid[1]
E'en on death's plain, A dreader curse is mine,
Who seeing saw not, hearing would not hear.'

    Such cry is on thy wave, O Galilee!
Nor there alone, where on thy western plain
The sower went to sow, and the seed fell
In stony places, and among the thorns,
But far and wide it wails from shore to shore,

---

[1] 'The name, perhaps even the remains, of Sodom, are still to be found on the shores of the Dead Sea, while that of Capernaum has, on the Lake of Gennesaret, been utterly lost.' Stanley, p. 374.

From solitude to solitude of mount
And vale and waters.
                          'Beautiful in death,'
Men call thee: and I know a silence lies
Shroudlike around.
                    Yet they do err. O be
For ever to my soul a sea of life!
Harp[1] of the Holy Land, from whose sweet strings,
Touched by God's finger, living music thrilled
His Holy Church, to me be never dumb!
Oh nay, thy numbers do not sleep or die!
Immortal must thou be, Gennesaret!
Still are the gifts and calling of thy God
Without repentance! Live as thou hast lived
Elect and loved by Him, Who was the Life,
And is, and is to be. He loved thee well
And His is love for ever.
                            I will stand
Upon thy shores and see, for all the thorns,
The goodly ground wherefrom there sprang life's fruit
An hundredfold: there were who heard and saw,
Nor found the saying hard, the vision dim,

---

[1] 'The real shape of the sea is not so much oval as harplike.'—See Macgregor, p. 326.

And lo! their sound is now in all the earth,
Their words in all the world.
                            Him I behold
Who here forsook his gain and set his lip
First to the Gospel clarion: at whose call[1]
The Morians' land stretched out her hands to God;
I see thy fishermen that evermore
Should win a nobler prey. Here Andrew brings
His brother to the Lord; here Philip calls
The guileless Cananite; and they are here
The Sons of Thunder. Warriors, princes, priests,
These are thy children, and their glory throws
Rays of its life on thee.
                            The winds that blow
About thy borders, as I stand and gaze,
Shall whisper other than the sounds of doom;
And I shall hear the words that cannot die—
Wiser than sage's wisdom, poet's song,—
The words of that most sweet philosophy
That spake o'er all the melancholy waste
Of this world's sins and woes, 'Come unto ME,
All ye that travail: I will give you rest,
Ye heavy laden.'

[1] Africa is the traditionary scene of the missionary labours of St Matthew

Then I will go up,
And get me to the stronghold of thy hills,
A prisoner of hope. On solemn height,
In still ravine—the midnight oratories,
Or ere His glory, of my great High Priest—
I too will pray that He will plead for me
That my faith fail not; that I too at last
Through Him may rise further than faith and
    hope
To see the blessed vision of His face
Within the gates of praise.
                      Or on thy waves
Sometime my soul shall wander:
                          First at dawn
After the night's vain toil, I shall behold,
On the white shore, in His 'meek majesty,'
My Lord draw nigh: and my poor ship shall be
His high cathedral throne. Then at His word
I will thrust out and find in the glad morn
Exceeding great reward.
                      Or I will dare
At His constraint the peril of the storm—
When behind Tabor dies the light away,
And from some gorge of Bashan rush the winds,

Or floodlike[1] on the floods from heights of air
Shall in great wrath come down—then at my cry
Out of His tranquil sleep He will arise
And 'Peace, be still!' shall bring the calm of Heaven
Instant on wind and wave.
      Or it may chance
In the deep night I toil in middle sea.
'Tis wild and chill: no balm comes off the shore
Beneath the moon from far Gennesaret,
No nightingale is heard from garth or glade,
No sound in pauses of the baffling wind
Falls faint or full, save the hyæna's scream,
Or some demoniac's howl in Gergesa
Among the tombs; and my heart droops in me:
Then, lo! an awful Presence breaks the gloom,
Walking the waves, and a voice, solemn, sweet,
Stills my heart's sudden terror, 'It is I:
Be of good cheer!' and lo! it is the Lord,
The Very 'God Whose way is in the sea,
Whose footsteps are not known,' Whose love shall
  bring
My weary soul at last where it would be.
  Once more thy waters bear me, and again

[1] "There came down a storm of wind." St Luke viii. 23; and cf. Macgregor, p. 421.

After a barren night a cheerless morn.
Heavy my heart; for though my Master lives
He is not here: and my remorseful soul
Cries, 'Thou hast lost thy Saviour by thy sin.'
Low lies my boastful pride: and as I hear
Through the dim dawn, 'There cast and thou shalt
    find,'
I will obey, not question.
                      Lo again
The morning miracle. It is the Lord!
I get me to Him, for I needs must go!
Though I have sinned, and I have lost His love,
I love Him and must go. He bids me come,
He hath a feast prepared; He bids me eat,
And all amazed, and torn by hope and fear
I take the mystic food.
                      O then His eyes
Look on me; O divine, pathetic eyes!
All pity and the tender sweet reproach
Of love that never fails, and pardons all,
Gaze on me there—and for the memory
Of each dark sin, He has but this one word,
'Lovest thou ME?'
                    Yea, Lord, Thou knowest all;

Thou knowest that I love Thee.
                              Yet there comes
One other word—last legacy of love
Which I will keep for ever to that end
Of which He spake,[1] the happy awful end—
'Follow.'
              Yea, Master, Saviour, Lord and God,
Thee will I love and follow to the end.

[1] 'This spake He, signifying by what death he should glorify God.'—St. John xxi. 19.

The Gate of Death.

'Grant, O Lord, that through the grave, and gate of death, we may pass to our joyful resurrection.'—*Collect for Easter Eve.*

THE watching Church was near her Easter hope;
    The waiting earth was close upon her spring,
Soft breezes wooed the woodland buds to ope
        And woodland choirs to sing.

Yet was not Lententide nor winter past,
    Still were the lands of leaf and flower forlorn;
And Christian souls kept one more quiet Fast
        Or ere their Festal Morn.

It was Death's hour: but close are Death and Life:
    The long loud storms had breathed their latest breath;
In dying is the agony and strife,
        But solemn peace in Death.

So had the awful Friday passed in pain,
    And souls were calm that had not ceased to grieve,
Since in their sorrow Hope drew close again,
    Again with Easter Eve.

One lay and waited as the hours went on,
    Watching the shadows deepen round his bed:
One whose long Lent of life was almost gone,
    And winter well-nigh sped.

Spring was so near him, and the glorious Feast;
    And his believing soul in calm foretaste
E'en in that death-hour from all trouble ceased,
    Nor needed to make haste.

And one was watching with him, young and fair,
    But fairer than in beauty of her youth,
By that sweet patience which meets earth's despair,
    Secure of Love and Truth:

His Love, His Truth, Who cannot change or lie,
    Lover of souls and LORD o'er Death and Hell;
Who saith, 'In Me all things below, on high,
    For you are always well.'

Her heart was full of tears, and almost rent,
    Well-nigh too full for life, yet her child's will—
A will not lost but with her Father's blent—
        Lay satisfied and still.

Husband and wife: so dear, so near, that earth
    Had naught for each without the other good,
Yet son and daughter by one heavenly Birth,
        Beneath one Fatherhood.

And heaven is more than earth, and so their love
    Was more than earthly, even as their life—
In souls so sure of hidden bliss above
        No sorrow grows to strife.

' My children do not part, and cannot die:'
    Yesterday taught them by the Cross in sight,
To-day by that dark Sepulchre hard by,
        Morn by its promised light.

She sat beside him till the night grew deep,
    Her eyes on his, his hand within her hand,
The perfect peace she saw had power to keep
        Her own heart in command.

Not much they said: Love unto love can tell
   Its inmost feeling, though of words be none,
By look, by touch, in thought they commune well,
   Whose heart and soul are one.

Yet, twice he spoke: once, when as day grew dim,
   And a bell ceased upon the still March air,
She sang the Church's Psalms and one sweet hymn,'
   And prayed the Vigil Prayer.

Then first he said, '"The Grave and Gate of Death"
   Are near this Eve: LORD! let my soul be borne
Through them to Thee with the first light and breath
   Of Thy victorious Morn.

'I will "remain in patient watch" till day—
   This gloom is holy, for it once was Thine—
Then, O my Righteousness! with Thy first ray
   Bid me arise and shine.'

Again was heartfelt silence for an hour;
   Then one came in, whose voice well-known and dear
Brought prayer and counsel and the Word of power
   The contrite love to hear.

' See *Hymns Ancient and Modern*, No. 10

Beautiful were his feet. When he was gone
    Light seemed to linger and the calm increase,
Flowing from those last words, the benison
    Of the eternal peace.

The hours crept on: till dawn was close, and still
    She watched beside him. Once she thought he slept,
Nor knew but it was death, and then her will
    Failed in her, and she wept.

No sound, but tears upon his hand could tell
    Her anguish; and, with love that could not chide,
He whispered, 'Dearest, even this is well,
    HE wept when Lazarus died;

'He knows His sheep; God-Man; and in His ears
    Your cry is holy; even *Hope* can weep:
"I go," He said, and went, amidst His tears,
    "To wake him out of sleep."

'Like Him you weep—and I—O love, my wife,
    I weep too!—but our tears do Faith no wrong,
The heirs together of the grace of life,
    Our parting is not long;

'Yet now we part; and e'en the "little while"
  Seems long to love: but oh! if life is sweet,
Sweeter it is to lay it with a smile
      At our dear Master's feet.

'My darling, this is all; speech fails; stoop low,
  Tenderest face I love so!—now, before
Sight, sense, fail also, and I cannot know
      Even you—kiss me once more.'

She kissed him. O how piteously her soul
  Longed to go with him, even while its cry
Lay hushed in reverence, for its trust was whole
      In its great agony.

She kneeled, her arms about him, by the bed,
  And watching the dim eye and fitful breath,
Seemed with her still white face beside his head
      A very Bride of Death.

Slowly the darkness shrouded all the room,
  As the spent fire and watch-light died away;
Slowly again came creeping o'er the gloom
      The sense of the new day.

A low broad window looked toward the East;
   And as a hand before a taper's gleam
Glows red, its curtain folds, as dawn increased,
      Veined with rich life did seem.

His face was from it: but in fear anon
   She saw his spirit saw, by the set eyes,
The loosened clasp, the gesture as of one
      Preparing to arise;

Then one faint sign; whereat—as if she knew
   Behind it all the Beatific Sight
Lay veiled—with awful hand she backward drew
      The curtain from the light.

Blest Light, blest Morning! beautiful it shone
   Just over the dark hills with orient rays,
Which, like the summons from a trumpet blown,
      Poured full upon her gaze.

He slowly turned to look from where he lay:
   Then once or twice, like one most blest, he sighed,
Then laid his pale hands close as if to pray,
      And, gazing still, he died.

CHRIST'S Morning! ceased before it the old law
  That bound in prison-house the yearning soul,
Which fled to taste the glory that it saw,
  Freed from its long control.

'Dimittis, Domine!'—was that the prayer?—
  'Here have I seen Thy Promise, Risen LORD;
Now I depart to find Thy Fulness there,
  According to Thy Word!'

. . . .

And she?—she waits; alone but not forlorn,
  And learning more to long as less to grieve,
Keeps, with an ever brighter hope of morn,
  Her quiet Easter Eve.

The Birdie.

FROM his short slumber in the early morn
　　The sick man woke. Beneath the window sill,
Caged in this alien land, an English lark,
Making melodious prelude to the light
Ere the dark shades were driven all away,
Lightened its exile with the songs of home.
Strange in that land,[1] alone of all its kind,
Well was 'the Birdie' known for leagues around;
Rough men, uncouth in look and speech, would come,
As those who keep a Sabbath after toil,
And hush their ribald blasphemies, as though
They stood in holy presence while it sang;
And their wild faces would take back again
Some looks of childhood and those purer days
Far off, or ere the branding lust of gold
Had marred them.

[1] Elihu Burritt tells a story of the intense interest excited among the colonists of an Australian settlement by the singing of a lark—a bird not indigenous to Australia—kept in a cage outside her window by a widow. She had brought it over from England to share her exile, and refused all the many offers of purchase made to her.

On this morn the Birdie's note
Woke from his fevered sleep the dying man.
He knew the time was near that he must die:
And, smiling as the broken-hearted smile,
He said in thought, 'This wide Australian land,
That never gave me welcome to her arms
Or bade me find a home upon her breast,
Will open soon her heart and lay me there,
And suffering none to break my quiet sleep,
There she will clasp me closely till the end.'
Was it not hard to die so far away
From all of place and person that he loved?
To die alone, not one of all his kin
To minister the last necessities,
To fan the burning fever from his brow,
To cool his hot dry lips, and, more than all,
To give him tender words and loving looks.
And make death calm and holy—as a wind
At even, breathing softly from the west,
Gladdens the dying sunlight, or as when
It breathes like pity through the autumn woods,
And the sere leaves like dying hopes float down
Gently to their decay, not torn by gusts
Nor whirled away in tempest—even so

To breathe upon him all the gracious air
Of reconciling sympathies, and then
To close at last the sightless eyes, and then
To shroud the still cold form, and reverently,
As one who sows immortal seed for God,
To lay it in the furrow of a grave,
Waiting His golden harvest, over it
Dropping the precious rain of holy tears.
Not one—and yet how might he call it hard?
No other hand than his had cut the bonds
That bound him to his kin and to his home.
Nor might he rail against the land he loved
And longed for far away; nor stern nor cold
Had been its motherhood to him her son,
But kindly, as a mother, she had given
All liberal gifts to meet a modest need,
And yet, as one too wise in love to spoil,
Withheld her treasure from his grasp. But he
Had heard a siren-call come o'er the waves
From the great Golden Isle, had seen in dreams
A glorious Spectre clothed in sheen of gold
That motioned him to follow; unto whom
He said, 'I follow,' and arose and went.
Went—careless of the dear familiar land,

Heedless of loving eyes that wept for him,
Deaf to the tender voices praying him,
Scornful of Duty with her stern reproach,
'Stay, for thy place is here,'—and more than all
Striving to cover what he could not hide,
A Form with Arms outstretched to draw him near,
To deaden that within which would not die,
Another, 'Follow Me, for thou art Mine.'

  O'er the long leagues of that sea waste between,
Cursing the tardy hours that would not fly
And bring him face to face with all his hope
Quick as his eager longing, on and on
The gleaming Spectre lured him; till it stood
In that far land which seemed another world,
And bade him come and thrust his greedy hands
Into that treasure-heap. It is a tale
Oft told, yet not too often. While he grasped
There came against him surely one by one
Avenging powers to hinder: pains of toil
Unwonted, hateful scenes of sin and strife,
The savage life beneath the burning sun,
The broken sleep of fear beneath the stars,
The want of better things than gold, and then
The robber's cruel hand that made in vain
Long weary months of labour, then disease,

And with it none to heal and none to cheer;
And so it was that ere a year was gone
He saw that golden phantom, as a cloud
Tinted by sunset lapses into gloom,
Slow darken into grisly hues of death.

    And now it was that memories of home
And those fond hearts that waited wearily
Beyond the evermore-dividing seas,
Came thronging in sweet sadness over him,
With holy influence from the Source of love
Moving his soul to prayer. And so the Form
Which he had sought in vain to see no more
Looked also down upon his heart in love,
Not in reproach: he thought those gracious Arms
Leaned to him from their Cross of pain as though
To draw him near for blessing; and a Voice,
Rich with the eloquence of mercy, seemed
Ever to fall more clearly on his soul
'Ere long thou shalt be with Me—thou art Mine.'

    And on this early morning as he lay,
Yet clearer, nearer seemed to fall that Voice,
'This day thou shalt be with Me,' and his soul
Made answer, 'Yea, since Thou forgavest him
Who died that day, I, though more vile than he,
Will hope for mercy greater than my sin.'

And as he lay and brighter grew the morn,
And sweeter sang the Birdie—while a sense
Of pardon calmed the waters of his soul
Into a perfect stillness—on their breast
Came mirrored from the old beloved land
Scene after scene of other days long dead:
Came not to trouble but to soothe, and all
Seemed wrought to real life as by a spell,
And the spell-worker seemed the Birdie's song.

O sweetly, sweetly rang the joyous note!
He thought he was a child again, and stood
With others, children also, by a stream
Which, as it were the type of their glad lives,
Ran, making merry music through the fields,
Ran, with a rippling welcome and farewell
To every blossom met and left behind,
Ran, careless of the solemn mystery
Of ocean ever nearer day by day.
So sped he with his fellows by the banks
And through the meadows, greeting hastily
All bonny things and bright, and stayed for none.
Heeding no future save the next hour's play—
And round and o'er him laughed the frolic wind.

O sweetly, sweetly rang the Birdie's note.
And now he was a boy whose eager heart

Would fain in this the glimmering dawn attain
Manhood's full day: with visionary eyes
Blending his future with the glorious past
He saw no present: all the quiet hills
About his home were castled heights of war,
And down their placid sides his fancy scanned
Descending squadrons sweeping to the fray.
The keen fresh morning breezes woke his soul
Like battle clarions; peaceful woodland scenes,
Through which the simple cotter wound his way,
He peopled from the noble names of Eld
With warrior forms: Great Arthur, flower of kings,
True friend and terrible foe, rode there; and there
Sir Galahad, who sought the Holy Grail,
With earnest face and pure; and here was heard
Sir Roland's horn: and ever there and here
Some immemorial deed was wrought again.
These faces and a thousand else he saw,
He saw them all and loved them, and he longed
To follow and be like them; and the sun
Shone brightly o'er him, and the blackbird's call
Came to him like a bugle from the dell,
And all things seemed so beautiful and true,
He cried aloud until the echoes rang—
And round and o'er him swept the rolling wind.

O sweetly, sweetly rang the Birdie's note.
And now the scene was changed, and still alone,
Yet not alone, for there is life in death,
He stood beside a grave. Not many years
Had made him older since that day, and yet
Not one expectant glance in those dim eyes,
Not one bright gleam upon the stricken face,
Alas! not e'en toward Heav'n; he stands and looks
A stony look beneath, and bitter words
Low-voiced with sullen passion made their way:
'I loved her with a love that made me pure,
And she is gone; the truth was in her eyes,
And they are closed for ever; her bright hair
Made chains to bind me to the hope she held
Of God and angels; they are loosened chains
There in the dust. She was my all in all,
Truth, Honour, Beauty, Purpose, Purity,
Hope, Joy, Faith, Comfort—all—and she forsooth
Was needed elsewhere and not left to me.
And I go forth and care not where I go!'—
And round and o'er him sighed the ghostly wind.

    Yet sweetly, sweetly rang the Birdie's note.
Cloud-like the sin of those remembered words
Troubled the vision of the dying man.
A moment—and it sped, for now no more

Came memories of the past; a marvellous light
Such as he knew not, drowning all the morn,
Flooded his soul, and music wonderful,
In which the Birdie's warble blent and died,
Began, rose, swelled and deepened into Heaven
Louder than loudest thunders, yet more soft
Than all earth's sweetest silence. Then a form,
Bright from God's presence, hovered down and
  smiled—
And yet he knew it—and a voice he knew,
Attuned to that strange music, flowed to him,
'Arise, come hence, beloved! I am sent
To bring thee, for He calleth thee, and now
Thine eyes shall see Him—Come.'
        Before the day
Shed its full lustre, one who slept beneath
Woke with a sudden start, and knew not why,
But rising quick, and coming half in fear
Within that chamber, he beheld his face
Shine with a light which was not of the sun,
Nor yet of inner life, for he was dead;
Dead—yet without, as though there were no death,
And as its music had been learnt in Heaven,
Sweeter and sweeter sang the Birdie still.

What the Mountain said to the Maiden.

AND must the mountain speak to thee, O Maiden,
    To thee among the lowlands far away?
I with the weight of solemn ages laden,
    Thou in the freshness of a first spring day.

Full many they whose gazings fall upon me,
    Curious or careless, and no word say I;
No power have they to cast a glamour on me,
    And, dull of head and slow of heart, go by.

Most rare the spell, and yet from thee I know it,
    So must mine ancient silence cease for thee;
For thou hast cast thy glamour on my poet,
    And he, my master, casts his spell on me.

And I rejoice; my poet is my prophet,
    The power I bend to doth my head upraise:
I know the sweetness as the sternness of it!
    The priest of nature wakes the world to praise.

He said, 'O mountain, shall my lips adjure thee,
   By thine allegiance to the kings of men?
Or by a promised guerdon shall I lure thee,
   Thy name writ grandly by a poet's pen?

'Howbeit, open out thy heart's deep treasure,
   There dwells a little maiden in the south:
I bid thee, for her profit or her pleasure,
   Drop some rich word of wisdom from thy mouth.'

But what have I to suit thine ear, O maiden?
   Wouldst thou some wild apocalyptic word?
Wouldst learn the secrets of my mystic Aidenn,
   And hear the sternest music ever heard?

Nay, child, not for thy gentle eyes such vision,
   Weird faces, flame-like hair, and dismal forms,
Not for thine ears the wrath and the derision
   That meet and mingle in the voice of storms.

Not this my tale to thee; no vision mystic,
   No sounds of war to vex thy spirit's calm,
Yet wilt thou lose no majesty—majestic
   Beyond all pæans is the Church's psalm.

The Church's psalm of peace ; the joy, the beauty,
    Of lowly lives ; the loftiness of love,
The deep light glowing on the ways of duty ;
    The voice and presence of the holy Dove.

Thereof I commune when the priestly morning
    Lays first on me the great day's crown of light,
Or when I robe in even's rich adorning,
    Or reign sole monarch of the realm of night.

Thereof I commune, and I know the splendour,
    Earliest and latest, which I thus have worn,
Exalts me not ; my rocks are not more tender,
    And my lone grandeur is not less forlorn.

Low lie the valleys, and I tower above them,
    My bended head is close beneath the sky,
Yet with meek reverence am I fain to love them,
    For they are dearer to my God than I.

Dearer to God—to them His grace is given ;
    Mine the storm-torrents and the warring gales,
And wild birds, songless ; theirs the breath of heaven,
    Flower-fostering fountains and the nightingales.

And if my word be of mine exaltation,
   Take up thy parable and say, 'He stands,
This Pharisee of hills, with vain elation,
   In that great Church which is not made with hands.'

Nay, rather be it, 'See the mountain hoary,
   Showing the track which children's feet have trod,
Saith, in the valley is the path of glory,
   For this world's lowliest are the great with God.'

Yea, none but valley pilgrims find the fountain,
   Whence with absolving waves life's river rolls,
And only they shall climb at last that mountain,
   Where God hath set the Eden-land of souls.

Leave then the summits to the storms, sweet maiden;
   On! through the quiet valleys of the earth,
Till thou inherit in the heavenly Aidenn
   The mountain glories of thy second birth.

The Maiden's reply to the Mountain.

O LORDLY mountain, to thy salutation,
    Greeting so tender from a throne so high,
The maiden meekly from her lowly station
    Far in the southern valley makes reply.

As thou didst speak I answer by my poet:
    My heart as thine be open to the seer!
Truly I feel thy glory, he will show it:
    My wordless musings let his song make clear.

Thy glory? yea, I know it sets me higher
    To hear of thee or see thee in my mind:
God's grandest creature—grander than His fire,
    Ay, than His ocean or His ocean wind.

Grander for though to thee no beauty vernal,
    Or bloom of summer give a single flower,
Yet the Lord God hath written thee 'eternal,'
    And stamped thee with the signet of His power.

Who knows but in the great regeneration,
    When He shall make the whole world new, that thou
Shalt only change, erect in thine old station,
    By bloom and beauty which thou hast not now?

Thou and thy brethren (as round Zion olden
    The hills were marshalled, frowning back her foes,)
Standing about Jerusalem the golden,
    Majestic columns of her sure repose.

Then beautiful unspeakably—not hoary
    With barren snows or dark with giant glooms,
But robed in splendours of unfading glory,
    Enwrapt in music, incensed with perfumes.

Yet dearer now, more awful and less splendid,
    Art thou to us in these dim years of time,
For till the mysteries of life be ended
    That is most precious which is most sublime.

Oh, thou dost teach me: ere the consummation,
    The highest is the hardest, the most bare:
Here a sad Hill beheld His tribulation,
    For Whom the gates of glory opened there.

And we go after: up the height of sorrow:
　　We are but strangers, and we seek our rest,
And soonest on that height shall break the morrow,
　　And nearest there the kingdom of the blest.

Ye hills, ye seem the great earth's aspirations,
　　The heavings of her full heart toward the skies!
And so, sublimer are the soul's sensations
　　That lifts to *you* her meditative eyes.

And as she muses, how with rolling thunder
　　And sweet harp-music on her memory throng
Undying names, and poet-words of wonder
　　From holy annals and prophetic song!

Now she beholds with awe th' uplifted token,
　　Ensign of wrath or love, the sovereign rod!
Now hears with joy what glorious things are spoken
　　Of Zion, mountain-city of her God.

Borne on the eagle's wings of spirit vision,
　　And rapt into the past she takes her stand
In the dim twilight of the old religion,
　　Amid the mountains of the ancient land.

And here she bows, in lowliest adoration,
    'Neath one great height hid in a fiery cloud,
What time outpeals, above a prostrate nation,
    The archangelic trump exceeding loud.

And there, where Nebo, like an old stern warder,
    Towers o'er the plains, by one still form she stands,
And gazes with him to the ocean border,
    And marks him stretch in vain his longing hands.

But she may pass; and o'er the sacred river,
    Whose streams make glad the valleys of the blest,
She wings her way where God has willed for ever
    The crown supreme of all His hills should rest.

There most she lingers where the great salvation,
    GOD's blessing in His Blood, fell like the dew;
Where found the holy Church her strong foundation;
    And the whole earth her peace and plenty drew.

Yet are there many mansions of His glory!
    Both North and South rejoicing in His name;
Tabor and Hermon, each with his own story,—
    All are as pillars of th' eternal fame.

From peak to peak, from altar unto altar,
    Height calling unto height, she speedeth on;
Nor do the fleet wings of her rapture falter,
    Up to the cedar crowns of Lebanon.

So is my spirit ever rapt and lowly,
    In visioned presence of the ancient hills,
As though the sacred words and footsteps holy
    Abode upon them yet in awful thrills.

Oh, Friend far off, for them do I revere thee,
    As for thyself, thou Teacher true and strong;
So with a grateful gladness do I hear thee
    Drop words of wisdom in my poet's song.

Sweet is the vale, thou sayest, O my mountain,
    And graces manifold its bosom fill;
But know I not that fulness hath its fountain
    In the deep heart of some eternal hill?

Vales of the wide earth all are Zion's debtors;
    Life's river sprang not from a lowly sod,
But, freed in season from its old-world fetters,
    Rolled to the valleys from the hill of God.

There we are come—not to the mount of thunders,
   And dreadful darkness, and more dreadful light,
But to the loftier hill of holier wonders,—
   Of Love, the breadth, the length, the depth, the height.

Thither we go; not yet our last endeavour,
   Not yet the helping hand of His last grace,
Have set our happy feet at rest for ever,
   There by the King our Father, face to face.

But soon; and though this hope soars far above thee,
   Yet does thy vision with its rapture thrill;
So must my spirit reverence and love thee,
   So with this song flies, bird-like, to the hill!

Trust.

'As thy days, so shall thy strength be.'—DEUT. XXXIII. 25.
'Trust ye in the Lord for ever: for in the Lord Jehovah
is everlasting strength.'—ISA. XXVI. 4.

O FELLOW-CHRISTIAN! whosoe'er thou art,
    This is for thee and me—
This wine of Trust, that maketh glad the heart
    In its adversity:
Drink, therefore, and so bear a braver part;
    For as thy days, thy strength shall be.

'Thy days' may be a life-long battle-field,
    A warrior's history,
Where every weapon Satan's arm can wield
    Shall each be aimed at thee:
But strive in Trust, and thou shalt *never* yield;
    For as thy days, thy strength shall be.

'Thy days' may be a weary pilgrimage
    Through wastes of poverty;
The vulture's hunger and the lean wolf's rage
    Be ever threatening thee:
Thy childhood joyless, and thy youth like age;
    Yet as thy days, thy strength shall be.

'Thy days' may be a voyage full of fear
    Over a stormy sea,
And thou the sleepless helmsman sworn to steer
    The good ship warily—
The sharp rocks there—the roaring whirlpool here—
    Yet as thy days, thy strength shall be.

'Thy days' may be a dull and vacant range,
    A long captivity,
Nought brightly wonderful or sweetly strange
    To quicken time for thee:
Less pain or more the only interchange;
    Yet as thy days, thy strength shall be.

'Thy days' may be a long experience
    Of much perplexity;
The light it longs for, amid clouds so dense,
    Thy mind may scarcely see:

Then on thy Father cast thy confidence;
    And as thy days, thy strength shall be.

O burdened sufferer in a world of woe,
    Thy sorrow's mystery
Shall pass: *believe*, and one day thou shalt *know;*
    Above thine eyes shall see,
Be not impatient of the veil *below;*
    And as thy days, thy strength shall be.

O wakeful toiler in a world of pain,
    A long rest waiteth thee:
Seek it not here, but bravely lift again
    Tired hand and feeble knee:
If thou wilt *trust*, thy Master will *sustain,*
    And as thy days, thy strength shall be.

Yea, fellow-Christian! whosoe'er thou art,
    It is for thee and me,—
This wine of Trust, that maketh glad the heart
    In all adversity:
Drink, therefore, and so bear a braver part;
    For as thy days, thy strength shall be.

Amen! until there shall be no more 'days,'
    Until the shadows flee,
Until the cloud be lifted from our gaze,
    Until in Certainty
Trust die, and Faith in Sight, and Prayer in Praise,
    In GOD'S ETERNITY!

Lententide.

A MEDITATION.

'Out of the Deep.'

FAIN is the wakened soul to try
    Her pinions in the golden sky
Of peace and pardon instantly:

But they are clogged by thoughts that fill
Her mind with memories of ill,
A worldly love, a carnal will,

And she is forced to sit and weep,
And watch alone in valleys deep
The darker shadows onward creep,

As though to whelm her in a tomb
Of utter spiritual gloom,
Foretaste of the eternal doom.

'My sin!' the low despairing sigh;
'My sin!' the exceeding bitter cry,
Out of those depths is heard on high:

Glad angels hear it where they stand,
And wait—a ministering band—
Their Lord's permission and command;

It comes—and swiftly, down from heaven
A light whereby that gloom is riven!
A voice of power and peace, 'Forgiven!'

O blessed voice! O living light!
To wake those silent depths, and smite
With beams of day the vale of night.

But, ah! not yet is peace complete,
The foemen, fiercer for defeat,
Strive to regain their ancient seat.

The world, forsaken, brings again
Its joys and cares: the Will would fain
Its realm recover and retain.

And though that Light still shineth clear
Through those new shades, and though the ear
Hears still that Voice it loves to hear

Speak, as of old, on Galilee,
'Peace:' yet, withal, the heart must see,
And hate its own infirmity:

And cries, as one who cries for breath,
Worn and oppressed, 'I faint beneath
The alien body of this death!'

'Tis well, for, otherwise than so,
The soul, disdaining to lie low,
A deeper depth of ill might know—

A darker gloom, a gulf more wide,
Because a self-exalting pride
Would thrust her further from His side.

Therefore, the Church, that she may lead
Her children Homewards, hath decreed
This Holy Season to their need;

Heavenwards, Homewards! through the dense
Dark clouds of sorrow, and the sense
Of present frailty, past offence ;

Heavenwards, Homewards! by the road
The poor in spirit ever trod,
And tread, in pilgrimage to God.

Heavenwards, Homewards! till they win
That blest inheritance, wherein
Is no more sorrow, no more sin.

Coming Holy Week.

'The Master saith, My time is at hand.'—ST. MATT. XXVI. 18.
'The spirit indeed is willing, but the flesh is weak.'—ST. MATT. XXVI. 41.

SOON will the Holy Week be here;
It is as if my Lord were near,
And, half in hope and half in fear,

I went to meet Him, so to be
A witness of the agony
And bitter passion borne for me.

'In hope' that so my soul may gain
Harvest of joy from seeds of pain;
That, flooding over heart and brain,

A deeper sense of sinful night
May drive me closer to the Light
To read His Love with clearer sight.

'In fear' lest even while I weep,
As once of old, forgetful sleep
Should o'er 'the willing spirit' creep,

And I should hear, as heard the Three,
Those words of chiding sympathy,
'Could'st thou not watch one hour with Me?'

Be Hope the stronger! O be Thou,
Dear Lord, the Guardian of my vow
To keep my vigil near Thee now:

Aid my 'weak flesh' this holy tide,
That I, despite or sloth or pride,
May watch and pray as at Thy side.   Amen.

Easter Eve.

A NIGHT of silence and of gloom:
My Master lieth in the tomb—
Mine was the sin and His the doom!

. . . . .

So on this awful eventide,
My self-trust gone, my wealth of pride
All spent and lost, I fain would hide.

And where?—Lo, on this Eve alone
I come with contrite prayer and moan
And lay me down before the Stone.

All is so still, so deadly still—
E'en that dread scene upon the Hill
Scarce shook me with so strong a thrill.

For Calvary had its jeering crowd,
My tears were check'd, my love was cow'd
My pride took courage 'mid the proud.

The soldiers sleeping heed me not,
Their vigil is perforce forgot:
The world is banish'd from the spot.

So here I weep—for none are near
To fill my craven heart with fear
Of some sharp gibe for every tear.

And the deep stillness hath a cry
Reaching my soul, and none are by
To drown it with their blasphemy.

It saith, 'O ingrate heart, for thee
The passion in Gethsemane,
For thee the scourge, the mockery,

'The scarlet robe, the thorny wreath,
For thee the load He sank beneath,
For thee the Cross, the Cry, the Death!

'Yea, all for thee! and having learn'd
How great that love was, hast thou spurn'd
The due of gratitude it earn'd?

'Thankless and cold! thy broken vow
Of love and service asks thee now,
Here at His tomb, what doest thou?'—

'Tis true—yet am I fain to come:
In grief I have no other home
But near Him, though 'tis near His tomb.

And as in self-convicted mood
On mine ingratitude I brood,
A Voice upon the solitude

Breaks, like a benediction near,
And through the darkness in mine ear
Whispers of hope, and not of fear:

'Yea, all for thee! and all to save!
Forgives He not as He forgave?
Died His Love with Him in the grave?'

So on this holy eventide
I lay me down as at His side,
And pray to die as He has died :

That I may rise to meet the strife
With this dead heart renew'd, and rife
With impulses of love and life.

But can it be with one so vain,
So weak, so fearful of disdain?—
' It can be ! by the right of pain,

' And curse, and cross, and this dark night !
Thou shalt endure through all the fight,
And as thy days shall be thy might.

' So shalt thou bear His flag unfurl'd,
'Mid ghostly foemen overhurl'd,
In fearless love before the world !'—

Then, blessed Master ! only Friend !
Be near, inspire, sustain, defend ;
In prayer I battle till the end.

Till on this Lenten night forlorn
There breaks the final Easter morn,
And the unsetting sun is born.

. . . .

So on this blessed eventide,
Here at Thy tomb, here at Thy side,
I lift one prayer, Abide, abide!

The old sweet prayer so earnestly
Pray'd one sad eve, and heard of Thee—
Abide with me, abide with me!

The Bird of Grace.

'And the dove came in to him in the evening; and, lo, in her mouth was an olive leaf pluckt off; so Noah knew that the waters were abated from off the earth.'—GEN. VIII. 11.

SOBBING against the mountain walls—
   Like some long dirge that flows and falls
     And fails not from the night
On to the night—a whole world's grave,
Slow ebbed the vast sepulchral wave,
     Beneath the lonely height.

Fell now upon the patriarch's ear
No cry without of prayer or fear,
     And on the wastes beneath
Thick mists profounder silence flung:
Dim ghostly veils that overhung
     A solitude of death.

'Twixt peak and peak the great Ark lay,
Pregnant with life for that new day
    Swift dawning over earth:
Womb of the world that was to be,
In hope's still travail patiently
    Waiting the hour of birth.

But long it lingered: more forlorn
Morn followed night and night the morn
    As each no token gave;
This calm upon the mountain's crest
Was wearier deemed than the unrest
    Of the tremendous wave.

Sealed were the fountains of the deep,
The flood-gates barred, the storms asleep,
    Yet word or sign was none
That said 'Baptized from sin and woe,
The buried earth re-lives, and lo!
    Its new day hath begun.'

No sign: across the waters' face,
From its vain quest the Bird of Grace

Resought the sheltering ark:
Only the carrion fowl flew on,
Or ghastly floating forms upon
 Folded its pinions dark.

No word: save one in every ear—
'Trust thou thy God'—as each could hear,
 The unseen wastes along,
Leaving not storm but calm behind,
The passing of that mystic wind [1]
 In equal stillness strong.

Yet six days more of watch and prayer,
And still no summons thrilled the air,
 No sign the vigil blest;
Then morning saw the Bird of Grace
Once more into the shrouded space
 Speed on its lonely quest.

Slow passed the morn, the noon, away,
And evening came to crown the day,
 Seal of the perfect seven,
And with it light that waxed anon
So full, so rich, the window shone
 As it were set in heaven.

[1] Gen. viii. 1.

Glad grew the hearts that watched within:
'Twas more than light that entered in!
    Pledge of a world redeemed—
Of life celestial poured beneath
Through mists of spiritual death—
    The blood-red glory streamed!

Nor only this the sign: behold
The tide of splendour as it roll'd,
    As from the heavenly shore,
In through the window-gate o'erhead,
The questing bird—her mission sped—
    Upon its bosom bore.

Her mission sped—for not in vain
Her wings had swept the wastes again,
    And, lo! the token green,
Proclaiming from her mouth new life,
And peace new risen out of strife,
    By happy eyes was seen.

O blessed Bird! O blessed Tree!
That sang aloud all silently

CHRIST'S carol on that eve:
O holy Olive, holy Dove!
Ye messengers of Life and Love,
    We hear and we believe!

Sin was and is, and death by sin,
And like a flood hath wrath come in,
    To make an end of earth,
But still One great Ark rides the wave;
The Church above the wide world's grave
    Awaits its second birth.

Tossed on the raging waters' breast,
Or on the barren rocks at rest
    She sighs in vigil long,
But through dark mists and skies o'ercast
Heaven's light prevailing wakes at last
    Her eucharistic song.

Her song of joy for life and love:
For in her midst the holy Dove
    The mystic Branch displays,
And fain her heart—though still it wait
Its supreme bliss—to antedate
    Its everlasting praise.

Abba! my Father, reconciled!
For all Thy Church, for me Thy child,
    So evermore provide
The Bird of Grace on happy wing
The Branch of life and peace to bring,
    With light at eventide!

The Answer of the Hills.

With 2 St. Peter iii. 10, compare Rom. viii. 19-21.

DEAR friends among the hills, I sit at home,
    Spending a leisure hour 'twixt toil and toil
Here in the east of Babylon, and think
How fair the mornings were a week ago.
It is, forsooth, September still, but not
The same September to my eyes and ears;
It is not bright, it does not blow; the eye,
Dismally peering towards the chimney-tops,
Sees nothing but a small and sickly sun,
Fog-stricken; for so soon the month of mists
Has sent his haggard herald from the swamps,
Though he be yet a five weeks' march away,
To bid us surely look for him; the ear,
Amid a medley of suburban sounds,
Catches not one of nature; joyfully
Would it exchange for such a calm as this—
Doleful and chill as if the air were dead—

The rush of autumn rains, or that wild roar
You wot of, such a madness of the winds
As made one night tremendous, and, alas!
Ruined far off[1] a wonder of the world.

   Yet memory holds most dear of all those days
The calmest; 'twas a day she will not lose
Till heart and mind have need no more to search
The stores of old delight for pleasant food
Or pastime. Such a day begins below,
In no faint foretaste, that eternal rest
Remaining for God's people. Far away
Seemed the sad world, behind the hills that stood
Shoulder by shoulder shining in their strength,
Gigantic warders of a quiet land;
Parted for pasture all the vales beneath—
The long drought over and forgotten—smiled
With faces fresh and fair, being full at heart
With gracious rains: the woodland on the slopes
Looked up with life renewed, rejoicingly,
As if it stood for praise. For here was peace
That was not idle sleep: too real a life,
Too great a gladness, mingled with the calm

[1] H.M.S. 'Captain' was lost off Cape Finisterre on the night of Sept. 7th, 1870.

For slumber; and the brightness was like song,
Wide, full, but all too fine for common sound.
A reverence seemed to temper all the joy,
And make it worship worthy of that Fane
Not wrought with hands, whose dome of infinite blue
O'erarched it all, as peaceful as profound,
Soothing the soul with vastness; as it were
God manifest in awful tenderness
Over His world.
    It was the week's first day:
And 'twixt the hours of morn and evensong
I lay before those hills, beneath that heaven,
Among the grasses by the church, and watched
And felt in all my soul that awfulness
And beauty of repose.
    One only thought,
A darkness and a discord, thrust itself
Into my musing, of that doom of fire
Which one day shall destroy all earth and heaven.
But oh, your green hills would not suffer it!
There was nor speech nor language, yet my heart,
As God did give them utterance, could hear
Their voice interpreting His word.
      But read,

Thus have I fashioned faintly for your ken
The form of my complaint and their reply:—

 The shining hills before me lay,
 My musing heart was fain to say,
 'I mourn, ye hills, the stern decree
 That saith, "Ye shall no longer be
   On that dread day
 When heaven and earth shall pass away."'

 The shining hills made calm reply,
 That fell upon my foolish cry
 Like words that silence, gravely mild,
 The fretful accents of a child:
   'Beneath, on high,
 God's work is good, and shall not die.

 'Though heaven above and earth below
 Shall share the universal woe,
 That doom of fire shall but destroy
 All that not ministers to joy;
   Yea, even so
 Full life and beauty shall we know.

'That end true glory shall begin,
That doom is but the death of sin,
That night is mother of the morn,
In travail ere the light is born.
  That woe shall win
A world that life *can* reign within.

'Eternal life! no bounded lease
Of hours of pleasure and of peace,
But joys of service and of rest,
Of blessing and of being blest,
  That never cease,
And only change by sweet increase.

'For, thinkest thou, shall then be dearth
Of aught of grandeur, beauty, mirth,
That now makes glad the sons of men?
Shall they not see their joys again
  At that dread birth
Which shall renew the heaven and earth?

'Yea, trust that He Who all began
Hath for the end His perfect plan;

His good gifts are for evermore!
Creation that in common bore
    The woful ban,
Shall fail not of the bliss, of man.

'God's pity left her to the race
He would win back into His grace,
His poet sweet, His prophet true!
He shall her youth with man's renew,
    And each tear's trace
Wipe ever from her glorious face!

'Then shall ye see the field, the flood,
The restful vale, the placid wood,
All that ye loved in all the land!
And we, whose "strength is His," shall stand
    As erst we stood,
As when of old he called us good.

'Then come! for supreme joy in woe,
Last triumph in last overthrow!
In all thy grace, in all thy power,
Come! O thou sweet tremendous hour,
    Come even so,
For heaven above and earth below.'

The Meditation of Isaac.

GENESIS XXIV. 62-67.

THE first sad hour that darkens life,
    The first sense of decay,
  The heart's first weariness or strife—
    This doom may long delay,
But comes at length—th' inevitable sign
Of what in us alone is deathless and Divine.

  Or soon or slow, th' apocalypse
    Of needs than earth more wide;
  Or soon or slow, in some eclipse
    Of pleasure, passion, pride:
Or soon or slow, it cometh sad and sure
To say, 'Naught can below suffice thee, naught
    endure.'

Our life's experience hath its birth
   In travail very sore;
We groan to find the fruits of earth
   So stricken at the core.
'Tis hard to waken from that childly dream
That made life's lovely flowers all amaranthine seem.

Yet it is well that out of youth,
   Though in amaze and fear,
We thus should waken to the truth—
   That secret sad—and hear
The voice that cries, 'O blind of soul and fond,
Thou dost but sojourn here, thy true life is beyond!

'Lo, thou art of eternity!
   What canst thou find in time
Wide as thy soul's immensity,
   Or, as its hope, sublime?
Grope not amid these wrecks, but on them rise;
Know thyself what thou art, an heir of yonder skies!'

Yes, it is well; for joy abides
   More steadfast if more grave;
The sparkling rivulet subsides
   Within the deeper wave;

In ways of prayer and larger thought we find
What bliss in strength of trust o'erflows a quiet mind!

   So doth a second life begin
     For him who doth not quail;
   New streams of comfort flow within,
     Though the old fountains fail:
And in the seeming waste new flowers upspring,
New trees their calm cool shade beside the waters fling.

   Fell upon Isaac's heart of old
     The sickening sense of pain
   That saw earth darken and grow cold,
     And knew that not again
Could time give back the summer sunny-warm,
Its thousand sparkling joys, its one belovèd form.

   His heritage,[1] the solemn field
     By Hebron's altar stone,
   A treasure in its breast conceal'd
     Which had been all his own—
Death's now, for ever; in that lonely cave
Seemed it with that dear form his heart too had
     its grave.

---

[1] The field of Machpelah, before Mamre or Hebron, was the first, and at that time the only, possession of Abraham in Canaan.

O mother's hand and voice and eye!
　　Cold, silent, dimmed away!
With them the glory seemed to die
　　Out of the golden day.
Drear looked the world, so beautiful before,
Wrapt in the mists of death and sorrow evermore.

Then was it well that other light,
　　Which is not of this sun,
Brought other knowledge into sight,
　　And that new life begun;
And in his father's Hope he learned to stand,
With eyes that looked in peace far o'er this border-
　　land.

Then all was well: less lovely now
　　Than in the gleam of youth,
Life set a crown upon his brow
　　More noble with the truth,
The strength of trust in one exalted aim,
A crown more sure than joy, more excellent than
　　fame.

Yet but a space did God withhold
　　That proven heart from joy,

And, where sad Hagar saw of old
    His grace by Lahai-roi [1]—
The well of Life and Vision—sent ere long
On that lone, silent tent new love in light and song.

So fell it in an evening hour:
    Slowly he passed aside,
And sought in peace the gracious power
    That falls with eventide:
Blest is the hour—than all the day more blest—
Breathing on weary hearts the benison of rest.

Rich lay the sunlight far and near;
    Through the great palms it shone;
Whispered the breeze upon his ear
    Its tender monotone,
As, the fair fields the Lord had blest among,
Rose through the calm, sweet air the lone man's even-song.

---

[1] Beer-lahai-roi (the Well of Life and Vision) was the scene of the revelation made to Hagar (Gen. xvi. 14), and it was beside it that Isaac afterwards dwelt with Rebekah.

Then lo! the answer of the Lord—
 What vision meets him there?
He knows it for the sweet reward
 Of sorrow, trust, and prayer;—
O maid, as thou didst leave,[1] forget thine own!
Lo! 'tis thy lord—be his, for ever and alone!

O glowing eve! O light of love,
 Deep, tender, and serene!
O Lahai-roi! O life above!
 O light of the unseen!
LORD! from the alien lands so call Thy Bride—
So lead her, bring her home at blessed eventide.[2]

[1] Cf. Ps. xlv. 10.   [2] Zech. xiv. 7.

The Bishop of Winchester.

IN MEMORIAM.

(*FROM 'THE GUARDIAN,' JULY* 30, 1873.)

ANOTHER beacon-light blown out above us;
   Another buoy-bell stilled upon the sea;
Another pilot of the hearts that love us
   Passed from our company.

Blown out, above the coast line frowning grimly;
   Stilled, o'er the fatal silence of the shoals;
Passed, from the few who watch for us undimly
   The Cynosure of souls.

An hour ago, and how the light was beaming
   O'er iron rocks in smile of tender cheer,
Or, bravely at our need, a pharos streaming
   O'er surging shocks of fear.

An hour ago, and as the tide flowed faster,
   And we by dim dread shallows swept along,
How in our ears full-toned against disaster
     Pealed out the stern sweet song.

An hour ago, and at the helm serenely,
   His steadfast eye upon the steadfast Star,
We saw him stand and, lovingly as keenly,
     Steer for the Haven far.

And now, and in a moment, is all ended?
   Gloom for the light, and silence for the sound?
And by that faithful presence undefended
     Sails on the Homeward-bound?

We see, hear, hold him yet! To our emotion
   Only a change of deeper awe is given;
Naught dies upon the spiritual ocean
     That had its life from Heaven.

Still do we see—not now the changeful splendour
   Lambent or sparkling, leaping through the night—
But the abiding glow, most deep, most tender,
     A great life's lasting light.

Still do we hear—not now the silvern laughter
    We loved to catch 'mid many a mightier tone—
But this—the golden cadence that hereafter
    All memory shall own.

Still do we hold—not now the presence human,
    Kind, fearless eye, frank hand, and vigorous form—
But, closer yet, the inner and the true man
    That steered us through the storm;

To guide us still who loved him! cheering, warning,
    Past rock and shoal, and through the blinding foam,
Until the Homeward-bound at the clear morning
    Shall be at last at home.

Ah, Saint, there are who in the heavenly places,
    After the Vision of the Form Divine,
Shall greet not one among the blissful faces
    More wistfully than thine!

A Sick-Bed Confirmation.[1]

PAIN is her portion: each day's work and leisure
    Is pain in sterner or in softer stress;
This is her only business, only pleasure,
    The greater pain or less.

Yet speak I as a fool: This straitened 'only'
    Forgets the new life and the nobler birth,
Leaves her outside the re-creation lonely,
    A stricken child of earth.

Nay, she hath other portion besides pain
    Through these unlovely days of less and more,
She follows after, for exceeding gain,
    One Who has gone before.

[1] This is a parochial sketch from real life, and the incident especially referred to is authentic. The sufferer, a young girl in the East End, was confirmed on her sick-bed by Bishop Claughton, Archdeacon of London, in April 1873.

A Sufferer too, named then 'The Man of Sorrows,'
    But 'King of Glory' now beyond the strife,
And from His Agony and Death she borrows
    Her hope of blissful life.

In gentle ward of this sweet Hope's enthralling,
    In pain abiding, she abides in peace,
Its patient prisoner, she awaits the calling
    Of final full release.

A child of God, an heir with Christ, she knows
    She shares with Him the travail of her days,
Sure in His Glory that the greater woes
    Shall be to greater praise.

Nor was The Son Who bore the great Temptation
    By Angels of his Father left alone;
Nor to this daughter in her long probation,
    Less loving grace is shown.

The Satan-haunted wilderness can enter
    With wants and fears within this little room;
So for her need such help from Heaven is sent her
    Can make the desert bloom.

So came there one commissioned by this place—
    Commissioned from the Lord's Ascension hour
By the unbroken lineage of grace
    And heritage of power—

An Angel ministrant; no wealth or station
    Made claim upon him from this door; within
Was needing him an Heir of Christ's salvation,
    And so he entered in.

'Peace to this house,' he heard the brief confessing
    The great 'I do': made for the Seven his prayer:
And leaning o'er this child of pain with Blessing
    The Lord of Peace was there.

O patient eyes, now filled with happy tears!
    Ye saw the great Rock's shadow in that hand
Shading the soul with peace from all the fears
    Of this the weary land.

Peace! for the past the Precious Blood's Remission:
    Peace! in the drought the Spirit's gracious rain:

Peace! fairer henceforth that far Country's vision,
    Where shall be no more pain.

'My happiest day,' she saith; by prone affliction
    Being thus more blest; ay, and more blest is he
Who, blessing her, hath won that benediction
    'Thou didst it unto Me.'

Songs.

The Beautiful Death.

(SONG OF A CAVALIER'S MOTHER.)

HE died the beautiful death,
    For the Church and the King:
Shall his mother shed a single tear,
While yet so proudly she can hear
    His war-cry ring—
So fiercely strong, so sweetly clear—
    'For Church and King!'

He died the beautiful death,
    My own brave boy:
And—break though it may in its desolate ruth—
Thy mother's heart for thy loyal truth
    Hath passionate joy!
Dead though thou art in thy strength and youth,
    My glorious boy!

He died the beautiful death,
    Last of his race:
I saw him slain from the castle wall,
The last and the dearest one left to recall
    His father's face:
The last and the noblest and fairest of all
    Of the ancient race.

But he died the beautiful death,
    For the Church and the King!
And none shall see me shed one tear,
While yet o'er sorrow my soul can hear
    The war-cry ring—
So fiercely strong, so sweetly clear—
    'For Church and King!'

Christ's Knight.

'The Sword of the Spirit.'
'For an Helmet, the Hope of Salvation.'
'God forbid that I should glory save in the Cross.'

A HELM upon my brow I wear,
    I wield in my right hand a Sword,
A Banner with device I bear—
    For Christ my Lord.

Armed with the Spirit, helmed with Hope,
    My great Cross standard wide unfurled,
I fail not, fear not, though I cope
    With all the world.

I battle to my latest breath,
    Then not my joys but labours cease,
And I am borne to life through death,
    Through war to peace.

The guerdon, then!—O hour most sweet,
    When I shall kneel for my reward
Before the Face, beside the Feet,
    Of Christ my Lord!

The Ebb of Tide.

THE little maid lay moaning,
    Late at the set of sun;
They told him 'She is dying
    Now that the day is done!'
But, listening by the window,
    He heard the full-toned roar
Of great waves plunging, plunging,
    All down the silent shore.
And to the watchers weeping
    'She cannot go!' he cried,
'The soul-call never cometh
    At flowing of the tide.'

The little maid ceased moaning,
    And darker grew the night;
They cried, 'She is not dying,
    She'll see the morning light!'

But he heard there by the window
　　The plunging waves no more,
But the waters washing, washing,
　　Like a lake upon the shore.
And he heeded not the watchers,
　　As hopefully they cried,
But said, with lips all trembling,
　　'It is the Flood of tide.'

The little maid lay sleeping,
　　Or ere the night was done,
They said, 'She will awaken
　　To new life with the sun;'
But he listened the deep murmur
　　The sighing night-wind bore
Of the waters sobbing, sobbing,
　　As they forsook the shore.
'Now pray the Lord Almighty
　　Upon your knees,' he cried,
'Oh, pray Him by His mercy,
　　For 'tis the Ebb of tide!'

Ah me! the world is evil,
　　And sick with care and sin,

And, sure, the Lord had mercy,
   Who left her not therein;
For with one cry, 'O Father!'
   She woke ere it was day,
And sighed and smiled; and, sighing
   And smiling, passed away.
And, sure, in life more blessèd
   Her sweet soul doth abide,
Where on the Sea of Jasper
   Is never Ebb of tide.

The Sea's Amen.

'THE morn is best'—his eager tongue
    Interpreted his happy eyes:
And o'er the waves his triumph rung
    To where he saw the splendour rise,
As light's blue tide 'gan roll among
    The floating islands of the skies.
'The morn is best,' he cried agen,
    And the glad waters sang 'Amen.'

'The noon is best'—he said the while
    He watched the tenderer deeper glow
From wave to wave, from isle to isle,
    Below, above, to fulness grow;—
The love-born beauty of his smile
    A darling secret seemed to know.
'The noon is best,' he said agen,
    And ocean rolled profound 'Amen.'

'Even is best'—he said, and sighed,
   What time there breathed an odorous balm
On airs that ever lived and died,
   A silence now, and now a psalm;
And prayer-like shoreward moved the tide,
   As shrineward, in the holy calm.
'Even is best,' he sighed agen,
And one long wave intoned 'Amen.'

'The night is best'—he said, when deep
   And dark upon the ocean's breast
A mystic spell of awful sleep,
   A death in hope, divinely blest,
Fell—and he could not smile or weep
   But only wait and be at rest.
'The night is best,' he said agen,
And dreary murmurs breathed 'Amen.'

'Amen:' it is the matin cry,
   Noon's anthem, and the evensong,
And night's refrain: afar and nigh,
   Through all the mystery of wrong—
'Amen,' 'All's well,' perpetually
   The grand response is borne along—
For life and death and life agen
'Amen, All's well:' 'All's well,' 'Amen.'

Children's Song by the Sea.

WE who sing beside the shore,
    By our grand orchestral ocean,
Tune our singing to his roar,
    Murmurous rest or loud emotion:
Fresh as in our fathers' ears,
    Rings his olden endless story:
Ancient monarch of the years,
    Young as in his primal glory!

Double lessons doth he give—
    Alternated for our learning—
Lessons how to love and live,
    Never trite, though still returning:
None as he so free and strong—
    So by strength our mighty Master
Teaches us to war with wrong,
    And to bravely bear disaster;

So he teaches at the noon
  In his loud majestic splendour;
Then in whispers 'neath the moon,
  ' Be ye lowly, loving, tender.'
That he sounds in notes of war,
  Waves magnificently rolling !
This in murmurs on the shore,
  Like the holy church bells tolling.

For the heart and head of life,
  These are lessons not for scorning :
For the rest and for the strife,
  For the evening and the morning :
He is worthy of our song,
  And our loyal hearts' devotion—
He, the tender and the strong,
  Brave and loving-hearted ocean !

The Harvest of Souls.

GATHER the Harvest in:
    The fields are white, and long ago ye heard
Ringing across the world the Master's word—
    Leave not such fruitage to the lord of Sin,
        Gather the Harvest in.

        Gather the Harvest in:
Souls dying and yet deathless, o'er the lands,
East, West, North, South, lie ready to your hands;
    Long since that other did his work begin;
        Gather the Harvest in.

        Gather the Harvest in:
Rise early and reap late. Is this a time
For ease? Shall he, by every curse and crime,
    Out of your grasp the golden treasure win?
        Gather the Harvest in.

> Gather the Harvest in:
> Ye know ye live not to yourselves, nor die,
> Then let not this bright hour of work go by:
> > To all who know, and do not, there is sin:
> > Gather the Harvest in.
>
> Gather the Harvest in:
> Soon shall the mighty Master summon home
> For feast His reapers. Think ye they shall come
> > Whose sickles gleam not, and whose sheaves are
> > thin?
> > Gather the Harvest in!

Lullaby of Life.

SLEEP, little flower, whose petals fade and fall
    Over the sunless ground;
Ring no more peals of perfume on the air—
    Sleep long and sound.
            Sleep—sleep.

Sleep, summer wind, whose breathing grows more faint
    As night draws slowly nigh;
Cease thy sweet chanting in the cloistral woods
    And seem to die.
            Sleep—sleep.

Sleep, thou great Ocean, whose wild waters sink
    Under the setting sun;
Hush the loud music of thy warring waves
    Till night is done.
            Sleep—sleep.

Sleep, thou tired heart, whose mountain pulses droop
   Within the valley cold :
On pains and pleasures, fears and hopes of life,
   Let go thine hold.
            Sleep—sleep.

Sleep, for 'tis only sleep, and there shall be
   New life for all, at day ;
So sleep, sleep all, until the restful night
   Has passed away.
            Sleep—sleep.

Sonnets.

The One Name.

*'Who is among you that walketh in darkness, and hath no
light? Let him trust in the Name of the Lord.'*—ISAIAH L. 10.

IN One NAME I have found the all in all.
   It is enough, and It will never fail.
  Here on the height, or there within the vale,
In this my strength I shall not greatly fall.
If on the dark hills here thy fears appal,
  O thou mine Enemy! or there assail
  My fainting heart, yet shall they not prevail,
For on the NAME thou dreadest I will call.
  Oh then rejoice not! for I shall arise,
And heavenly light shall stream across the gloom,
And heavenly music drown the voice of doom,
  And a most blissful prospect cheer mine eyes:
All from that NAME belovèd and adored,
Thy sweet great NAME, O JESUS CHRIST, my Lord.

Trust.

' He that believeth shall not make haste.'

TRUST is both sweet and holy, good and great:
   Holy and great by the Divine control
Of Self and Will, the strength of those who wait
   When 'Make thou haste' is urged within the soul.
And sweet and good by beauty of that peace
   Won in the press of battle: their heart-rest
Whose many sorrows though they do not cease
   Are yet breathed out upon a Father's breast.
So too 'tis deep and high; deep lie the springs
   That through the drought sustain the river's flow;
High, sunward, heavenward, mount the eagle's wings
   What time the sullen clouds are spread below.
Deep are the calm seas 'neath their stricken face:
High o'er the world of storm the stormless space.

Good Friday.

I.

OH! that this day on which my Surety died
    May humble me, and out of Self and Sin
So draw me upward, that I may begin—
Low at His cross, exalted at His side,
Beneath my burden and above my pride—
    Henceforth a lowlier, loftier life, and win
    The 'Go up higher,' and the 'Enter in'
Said only to the meek. O Crucified!
Whom only thus I know as afterward
    Risen also and Ascended: let Thy pains
    In Passion and in Death—while need remains—
With all my life, borne for my sake, accord,
    That I may rise o'er my dead self and be
    In heart, though here on earth, in Heaven with Thee.

The Same.

II.

'REDEEMED!' What voices mingle low and high
 Within the compass of the one word's sound;
Justice and grace, God's wrath, God's love, profound
Beyond all searching, in its utterance lie.
 O hear therein, my soul, the Victim's cry!
What time the precious Blood from every wound,
From breadth, length, depth and height, drops to the
 ground.
 Yet hear therewith the anthems[1] of the sky—
Song of the Elders and the mystic Four—
 Song of the many Angels round the Throne—
 Song of Creation! trinal song as one,
Love's Blessing evermore and evermore!
 'Redeemed!' how Earth and Heaven are in the word,
 Thy Cross, O Dying Lamb! Thy Crown, O Living
 Lord!

[1] See Rev. v. 8-14.

Easter Sonnets.

I. MARY MAGDALENE ON EASTER MORNING.

'LAST at the Cross and first beside the Tomb:'
   Love ere the dawn had been her guiding ray,
And now the twain had come and gone their way
Love still shone out amid the deeper gloom
Of that new loss which seemed a second doom.
   There last He lay: Love whispered, 'Linger there,'
   And e'en in Hope's eclipse forbade despair,
And could the dismal vacant depth illume.
   Then lo, the gleaming angels! and the word
'Why weepest thou?' Yet was she all unmoved.
Angels sufficed not for the Form she loved,
   Nor all their glory for the stricken Lord.
Herein was love; not Heaven itself can bring
Requital for the vision of its King.

The Same.

II. THE GARDENER.

SHE turned, and knew Him not. So dim her eyes
   With their long weeping; or not all withdrawn
  Yet hung the veil before the face of dawn;
Or was she holden from the blest surprise?
Howbeit, she knew Him not, and in surmise
   Saw but the Gardener; for around the tomb
   The garden-plots were breaking into bloom,
As Spring o'er prostrate Winter 'gan arise.
'With Spring he comes,' she thought, 'to train and tend,
   And to subdue.' Erring she did not err;[1]
The spiritual winter here had end,
   And Spring was come for all the world and her.
And He, the Gardener of the quick and dead,
In this new Eden bruised the Serpent's head.

[1] 'Profecto, errando non erravit.'—*St. Augustine*

The Same.

III. THE GREETING.

HE said unto her, 'Mary.' With one cry,
   And in one moment, she was at His feet.
Oh to her desolate thirsting soul how sweet
The calling! as to those in days gone by
His voice on the dark waters, 'It is I.'
   O great good Shepherd! so He came to meet
The sheep that cried to find Him—so to greet
Her for whose need he was unseen so nigh.
   He knows His sheep and calls them all by name;
They hear not others but His voice they know:
She heard and knew the calling sweet and low,
   And to His feet in reverent rapture came.
O my great master! thus and evermore
Thee would I seek and find, love and adore.

The Salutation of the Elders.

I.

'These all died in faith, not having received the promises, but having seen them afar off, and were persuaded of them, and embraced[1] them.'—HEB. XI. 13.

WITH lifted eyes, with longing hearts, with hands
   Stretched out, as men who greet their friends afar,
   Or pilgrims of the night their morning star—
Amid the bloom and glory of the lands,
Or in the flowerless solitude of sands,
   On the rich plains, or by the barren foam,
   'Mid woes of exile, 'mid delights of home,
In pastoral companies or warring bands—
   So stood the Elders: strangers everywhere
This side that Fatherland they could not see:
   Pilgrims, for ever constant to declare
They sought a place of immortality,
   A spiritual city beyond ken
   God built, prepared, and kept, for waiting men.

[1] More literally and significantly, 'saluted them' ἀσπασάμενοι

The Same.

II.

*'These all, having obtained a good report through faith, received not the promise, God having provided some better thing for us.'—*HEB. XI. 39.

So stood the Elders: yet their wistful eyes
   Saw not the vision here: they never heard
  Our revelation of the Living Word
In His Epiphany beneath the skies:
They saw not JESUS die, nor live, nor rise
   Back to the many mansions: that Return
   Left not to them the promises that burn
Within our hearts in earnest of the Prize.
Burn! is it so? O that this larger grace
   Of fuller oracles and clearer light
   To us, so slow to hear, so dull of sight,
Be not our shame before the Master's face!
   O that our hope, more blest, may closer cling
   About that coming City and our King!

The Small-pox in the East.

I. THE SISTERS OF MERCY.

THOU through this city-world late roaming wide—
   Thy presence ever ruin, often death—
Who here i' the East now choosing to abide,
   Wouldst poison all the breezes with thy breath:
Not all unchallenged dost thou work thy will:
   There have gone forth against thee many a hand
And many a heart, that in this hour of ill,
   When most men fly or falter, still withstand:
The Healer here, the soul's Physician there,
   And others, rank and file: and, if it be
That more for duty's sake these do and dare,
   Yet are there who most meekly, mightily,
Work but in love. Angels of this sad city,
Ye Sisters of St. Saviour's tender pity!

The Same.

II. CHURCH MINISTRATIONS.

THE powers of evil work unwittingly,
    Unwillingly, for good; that word's control,
'Thus far, no further,' holds them, like the sea.
    How often are they made to bless the soul,
While they beset the body with the woes
    Of some disease that warns the world away,
And opens doors and hearts long sealed to those
    Who watch for all whom earthly hopes betray,
The heavy-laden and forlorn, to aid
    And lead them, pointing upward. Many a home,
Brought by these powers into the darkest shade,
    Has seen a new and better sunshine come,
And learnt ere long this word of heavenly cheer,
'The world forsakes us, but the Church is here.'

The Same.

III. A PRIVATE BAPTISM.

ONE room and small, and yet the home of four;
   Of these, three stricken: there the young
      wife dead,
The babe, which but a week ago she bore,
   Here dying by its father; on the bed
Now and again weakly he strives to raise
   His marred frame, and bleared eyes that he may see
His motherless boy, and hear the words of praise,
   'We thank Thee for this child new-born to Thee,'
Said by the kneeling priest. The chrismal dew
   Shines, as the tears shine on the father's face,
Diamond-like 'mid dark disease. O true
   And precious tokens of the streams of grace!
As 'JESUS wept,' he weeps for child and wife:
And from His Side sees flow their second life.

The Same.

IV. DEATH AND LIFE.

HE 'groans in spirit,' for his wife and son—
    Sore troubled, like his Lord: he weeps and
        cries,
'I have lost her: yet, O Lord, Thy Will be done!
    And he—oh now within Thine Arms he lies,
Our Father, and I thank Thee; yet, I pray,
    Oh spare him! for my sight is sore and dim,
I scarce have seen my son.—What do I say?
    It may be, Lord, that Thou hast need of him,
That Thou wouldst have him for his mother's joy;
    Thou knowest, Lord, and doest always best;
She is with Thee; and if she wants her boy,
    Lord, take him! I will think of them at rest
Together: is he not more hers than mine,
Now that her home is this no more, but Thine?'

The Same.

V. THE THINGS SEEN AND THE THINGS NOT SEEN.

IN womanhood's first freshness blithe and fair
    At last week's Feast together. Now they lie
Together doomed. As he who marked them there
    Here looks upon the leprous change, a cry.
'O for one moment of my Master's power!'
    Breaks forth within him: 'O to say, "Be clean,"
And see them rise within the self-same hour
    As if this hideous woe had never been!'—
Hush, faithless servant, are the things not seen
    Hid from thy soul by horror on thine eyes?
Dost suffer any cloud to come between
    Thee and the everlasting verities?
Against a deeper woe, for higher weal
Thou *hast* His power; speak in The Name, and heal!

The Same.

VI. SPRING AND EASTER.

THE room is dark, and at the door is death;
    Sightless, and marred beyond all knowledge, there
His victims waiting lie: their labouring breath
    Makes the sole sound, and taints the heavy air.
What comfort?—Ah, my God! who doubt Thy truth,
    And mock our Easter hope, should enter here,
And see Thy Word in its immortal youth,
    Serene and strong in mastery of fear.
Without, the changèd season smiles and sings,
    For winter's tyranny is overpast:
Within, is risen with healing in His wings
    The Sun, whose sky no death-clouds overcast:
There, Spring-tide's promise of regenerate earth;
Here, Easter sunshine of the second birth.

The Same.

VII. HOLY COMMUNION.

A LITTLE while, O Death, a little while,
   Then may'st thou enter in and make an end—
An end of sorrows—enter with the smile
   Thou usest when thou comest as a friend.
A little while: for meet it is and right
   That first we feast together—we who stay
They that be passing—so to part at night
   Foretasting union in the new near day.
The woful scene, the sickening air, the gloom,
   Mar not this Feast: round this poor Altar-board
Good angels gather, and account this room
   A Gate of Heaven by Presence of the Lord.
A little while, O Death! then set them free
To find His Face beyond this veil and thee.

A Sunday Confirmation in an East-End Church.

I.

WITHIN, the sounds were all of praise and prayer,
   The old alternate music of the soul,
   Triumphant, tender: now the lofty roll
Of glad thanksgiving shook the sacred air:
Now the pathetic voice of need and care
   Wherewith in reverent trust the children cry
   Unto a loving Father here most nigh,
Albeit not far from each one everywhere.
Without, the sounds were all of shame and sin:
   The pleasure-seeker's laugh, the drunkard's song,
   The vendor's shout amid a careless throng,
By turns broke softly on the ears within;
   And they who heard did more devoutly pray,
   'LORD, arm Thy children for the evil day.'

The Same.

II.

SO must it be *without*, while Time shall be,
   The evil world of revelry and strife,
 Alluring or assailing every life
Hidden with CHRIST in GOD, perpetually
Shall rave around it like a troubled sea.
   So may it be *within!* till Time shall end,
   The holy Church till her dear Lord descend
Drowning that discord in her harmony:
Blest harmony of souls that love and long!
   The deep sweet minor of her lowly prayer
   Rising beyond the world and mingling there
With the full swell of her majestic song.—
   Child! let thy heart through all the blatant days
   Keep such an inner shrine of prayer and praise.

A Morning Present of Spring Flowers.

I.

THE East wind slept last night (O be its rest
    As deep as death and long!) and with the morn
The soft fresh breath of April from the West
    Came blithely whispering, 'Spring at last is born.'
I woke and heard it: longing to rejoice
    Yet did I listen with a faithless ear:
'Often the breezes have a mocking voice,
    Too glad the sound for truth,' said Doubt and Fear.
When, Ida, in there came so sweet a breath,
    And then so fair a vision, of your flowers,
I cried, 'O Doubt, I doom thee now to Death:
    These must be heralds of the happier hours:
Such sound and scent and sight do surely bring
Authentic proof of veritable Spring.'

The Same.

II.

AND after Spring, the Summer! Fair the scope
    For fancy now elate o'er Doubt and Fear.
'Flowers!' (I invoked them) 'of all love and hope
    The poet-prophets, sing the Summer near!'
O then no vague foretelling on my ear
    Sang the sweet season! by no faltering hand
    Was drawn the picture of the radiant land,
The bridal beauty of the golden year!
The richer glow; the deeper blooms; the fall
    Of shaded waters in the burning noon;
    The dreams of seas intoned beneath the moon;
The adoring night;—I saw and heard them all.
    And true or vain the vision and the word,
    Yet I thank God that I have seen and heard!

John Addington Symonds, M.D.

CEASED TO PRACTISE, 1869, DIED FEBRUARY 25, 1871.

✠

'They also serve who only stand and wait.'—*Milton.*

I.

TWO lives of service lived he—both to GOD;
    The first of many toils, through many years,
As, on the path the Master-Healer trod,
    He wrought for others' weal—dried others' tears:
The last, the shorter, but the harder one,
    In pain of patient waiting, a stilled life
Wherein his wistful eyes looked back upon
    That old belovèd path of splendid strife.
Both in one Wise Sweet Will accorded well!
    Now shall they strive who serve, now shall they wait.
Which was the noblest, who can surely tell?
    This only we know surely, both were great.
This life was grand in storm, and that in calm,
The first a Pæan, and the last a Psalm.

The Same.

II.

THE first, a Pæan of triumphant breath,
    Which sounded, like a clarion, jubilant,
A conqueror's march against disease and death,
    A self-renouncing true Crusader's chant:
The last, a Psalm, the song of skill and strength
    Sadly surrendered, of a will resigned,
That found its own pathetic close at length
    I' the 'I am happy' of a quiet mind;—
Such were his lives of service: such shall be,
    In interchange, a Pæan and a Psalm,
The twofold utterance of our memory,
    So proud and peaceful, so elate and calm;
And ever both to Thee, O God, shall raise,
Giver of Power and Peace, one song of praise.

Windsor Parish Church Reconstructed.

1 Cor. xv. 49.—Phil. iii. 21.

SO dull and drear and cold but yesterday,
   With raiment all unlovely round thy form;
Now fitly clad in beautiful array—
   True symbol of heart-worship bright and warm;
Then like an alien that had waited long
   And in a lonely darkness sadly sighed;
Now with an aspect eloquent as song,
   A type of the elect and glorious Bride!
Dear Church! 'tis passing sweet and passing strange
   To know the Then and Now—what was and is—
Praise to our Lord! for such shall be the change
   When our 'vile bodies' shall be like to His.
For thou art yet thyself, purged of thy shame
Our own Church still; the same, though not the same.

In Charterhouse Chapel.

ON FOUNDER'S DAY, 1872.

I.

SINCE I knelt here ten years have slipt away
   And four: and only this to me is strange,
  That only in myself appears a change:
All else that then was seems the same to-day.
Here are the antique gownsmen, worn and gray,
   'Codd Colonel' and 'Codd Captain,' each old face,
  Long passed, seems still to fill its wonted place:
And there behind me all the young array
   Stands as it stood on that last Lenten morn,
When here with eyes all dim I sighed farewell,
And heard each old prayer like a passing bell!
   Well—of those half-shed tears I think no scorn;
Unchanged in this at least, from boy to man,
That I am heart and soul Carthusian.

The Same.

II.

I LOVE the Domus. *Floreat!* though no more
   Shall be beheld again on Founder's day
  Those ancient faces and that young array
In most pathetic union as of yore,
Meeting together where they both adore:
   Yet shall it flourish: 'tis a green old tree
   Deep-rooted in dark earth, yet vigorously
Bidding its young leaves and new branches soar
  And find a rich fresh life and freer course
Above these misty depths in purer air:
So to be not less reverend but more fair
  By a departure which is not divorce.
Æternum floreas, Domus! there and here;
Be greater there—here evermore as dear.

To Windsor Cemetery on May-day.

I. THROUGH THE PARK.

WE five went blithely gravewards on May-day.
    Gravewards: but over us all Heaven in smiles
  Broke through the tracery of woodland aisles
And gothic cloisters green: For all our way,
As through a Church of Resurrection, lay,
    Under one dome, through pillars, arches, spires;
    Nor did we miss the chant of Easter choirs;
High in the dome the lark, upon the spray
    Linnet, merle, mavis; last, one nightingale
Sang his first anthem purely without fear
As sure of welcome in a poet's ear
    Sang in the sunshine o'er the sylvan pale.
Then, passing, we fulfilled our quest, and stood
By the green graves above the choral wood.

The Same.

II. THE CEMETERY.

AMONG the graves: but round us the sweet air,
 Sun-warmed and laden from the lilac's breath
With living odours kissed the mounds of death;
Flowers, diamonding the grasses here and there,
Stirred to the soft caress, and everywhere
 Was life, and warmth, and beauty, and repose;
 While in the midst the slender steeple rose,
A Mother's hand toward home, serenely fair.
 Now what thy victory, Grave, or, Death, thy sting
Unto her children?—One we met, well known,
Worn with long winter and aweary grown;
 Summer was mine, and four were in their spring;
But all were blithe: and in one shadowy spot
Smiled to our smiling the Forget-me-not.

The Same.

III. THE LITTLE CHURCH.

IF I forget thee, O thou lowly Shrine,
    Prefer thee not in Israel, let my voice
    Forget the power of song, no more rejoice
With reverence in the faculty divine.
Thine am I by first love, for ever thine.
    Thine by a new-sent Deacon's hopes and fears,
    A Priest's first consecration: by prayers, tears,
And travail known to God. And thou art mine
    By the true love of souls that cannot die:
Of some yet on their journey, as of those
Whose tired forms round thee here awhile repose,
    And wait the last Spring and the open sky.
Whose welcome, if I fail not by the way,
I shall not miss on the new earth's May-day.

Lord Derby.

'SANS CHANGER.'

He said, 'I see I am not wanted here;'[1]
    And, with a gesture that spake more than words,
Half grief, half scorn, this Peer, without a peer,
Passed from the midst of those half-hearted Lords,
Or foes, or friends; these were as those to him,
Together faithless to the Church of God.
No man drew Stanley from the path he trod
In truth and honour! Though his eyes were dim,
His soul was strong; and though his step was slow,
His hero-heart was still what it had been,
The knightly champion of his Church and Queen.
Ah, me, 'the last great Englishman is low!'
But true to man, since loyal to his Lord,
Dear is his memory, rich is his reward.

[1] Lord Derby's words as he rose and left the House the moment the compromise on the Irish Church Bill was announced. This significant act was his last in the House, for he did not enter it again.

Bishop Gray.

IN MEMORIAM.

✠

'As we drew near to the village the sun sank beneath Table Mountain amidst the most gorgeous clouds, shading gradually from dark purple to the most rich gold. I have never seen so fine a sunset in Africa. A still finer sunrise I once did witness in the Karroo. This evening seemed to me almost a prophecy of work done in that dark land, and the sun of my life setting. Would that it had been done better! God grant that when my sun goes down it may be amongst such radiant glories as that which the eye has this day beheld.'—*Extract from Bishop of Capetown's Journal, see Letter by R. H. F. in 'Standard,' Oct.* 8.

I.

THERE, in the solemn glory of the west,
    He read God's oracle of love and death:
Heard in the calm this voice, 'The master saith,
Now is the time at hand, and thou shalt rest;'
Then fell on sleep. O happy warrior, blest
By all the toil and tumult of a life
Spent in the very fore-front of the strife!
Confessor, soon to hear thy name confessed,

Among the white-arrayed before the throne,
By the dear Lord, for Whom, betrayed again,
'Mid friends' defection and the world's disdain,
How greatly didst thou dare to stand alone!
Most bless'd! for Heaven and earth shall pass away,
But not His Word, nor thy reward, O Gray.

II.

And now, or ere that sunrise of the End,
How sweet the glowing eve of thy repose
I' the spiritual land whose hills enclose
God's garden! through what valleys dost thou wend
With many a new and many an ancient friend,
Those other martyr-heroes of the past!
If there thou seest thine archetype at last,
Him of the North, how do your spirits blend!
Remembering how hard it was to dare
'Against the world,' and now before the Lord
Reckoning the sweetness of His love's award.
Have Cyprian, too, and Austin met thee there,
And given thee their great welcome, with one mouth
Hailing thee 'Athanasius of the South'?

III.

O rapt Elijah, might thy mantle fall
On other prophets of this silken time!
When few dare call a heresy a crime,
Though it impugn the very All in All;
When more ignoble fears our hearts appal
Than any perils of a brother's soul;
When all too seldom falls the thunder-roll
Of James and John, or that clear trumpet-call
Which, amid counsels soft or cynic sneers,
Ever with no uncertain sound alarms
The sleeping Church, and wakes her sons 'To arms'
Where the One Faith the Holy Sign uprears.
O that our cautious hearts from thee may learn
There is a time when true love must be stern!

Evensong,

IN LICHFIELD CATHEDRAL, ON THE FEAST OF
EPIPHANY, JAN. 6, 1873.

(FROM 'THE GUARDIAN,' JAN. 15 AND 22, 1873.)

I.

EPIPHANY had rung to Evensong,
    As with its inner glory, old and new,
The Minster filled awhile a stranger's view:
A little while, and yet, as life is long,
Will be its memory in its sweetness strong.
Here soared the nave in dim mysterious space
Of over-arching, never-ending, grace:
And there, within, beyond the white-robed throng,
Above the solemn Altar's double flame,
Crowning the carven wonder of the shrine,
Stood out against the dark the uplifted Sign
Of life and glory won by loss and shame.
Lord Christ! by merit of that shame and loss
For ever front our darkness with Thy Cross.

II.

And one,[1] no stranger but its child, was there,
Looking his last with love's peculiar pain
On the dear beauty of the antique fane,
The old beloved home of praise and prayer.
Sweet be its memory to him! sweet and fair:
Sweeter for pain, fairer because of loss!
O Selwyn, soldier of the Cross, that Cross,
Towards whatever dark thou needs must fare,
Shall surely front it with perpetual light.
And thus upon thee, in what alien isle,
On what far seas, thy Mother's holy smile
Shall look from Home serenely through the night,
Till on thy day of labour, brief or long,
Rings the Epiphany to Evensong.

III.

These are thy journey's bounds! From Fane to
    Fane,
From sacred Feast to Feast, from Home to Home.
Between them lie the wastes of land and foam,
With many an hour of labour, longing, pain,
But still the memory and the hope remain.

---

[1] The Rev J. R Selwyn, son of the Bishop, was present for the last time before setting out for his Mission work in the South Seas.

So shalt thou see behind thee and before:
Behind, this scene: in front, the Eternal door
Which opens to the 'more exceeding' gain
For which thou losest this. How fair and dear
In sight and sound is *this*, thou know'st, I ween!
But unto *that*, excelling though unseen,
Thy faithful soul devoteth eye and ear.
For they, who say and do as thou, declare
They seek a fatherland exceeding fair.

IV.

'From Fane to Fane': from this—a Holy Place
Where in symbolic miracles of stone
Beauty and Righteousness each other own
Dear, near, and chosen, in Divine embrace—
To That—Most Holy, where in boundless space
Is the One Temple of the Great Reward,
The Vision of the Blessed—God the Lord
To His elect revealèd face to face;—
'From Feast to Feast': from this Epiphany,
Promise and foretaste of the good to come
In That Apocalypse; 'from Home to Home,'
From this, where sweetest praises still must die,
To that, whose age of ages shall prolong
The undrooping rapture of its Evensong.

Midnight in London.

(FEBRUARY 24, 1873.)

> ' From many a nook unthought of there
> Rises for that proud world the saints' prevailing prayer.'
> (KEBLE.)

'I WILL not spare: within its circling wall
    Are not ten righteous.' So descending Hell
In flakes of fire on shrieking Sodom fell.
I see descending Heaven on London fall
To-night, in flakes of snow. No fears appal
Or eye or ear. Most fairly on the sight
Lies the great seamless garment of pure white.
A robe, like Christ's, on London robes it all.
And all is still, save for the watchman's tread;
And, at the day's first hour, the voice of time
Tenderly solemn in a steeple chime,
Like life's calm promise uttered o'er the dead.
Such is the scene; sure, for this wicked city
Christ's Church hath pleaded well the Eternal pity.

Worcester Cathedral.

(Reopened Wednesday, April 8, 1874.)

(FROM 'THE GUARDIAN,' APRIL 15, 1874.)

PSALM XLVI. 4.

God's River! The One SPIRIT,
  Grace of the mystic SEVEN!
From Seaward mountain Seaward,
  From Heaven, it flows, to Heaven.

I. As it Was.

FROM far Plinlimmon to the western sea,
  On to the western sea through many a mile
Of sound and silence—sound of many an isle
Shut in for toil amid the circling lea—
Silence of many a wold's tranquillity—
Flows Severn; and the cities proudlier smile,
And the still pastures softlier, the while
They hear him roll by watching tower and tree.

And men writ poems by his side : and one,
In days when hearts were simple and were strong,
Was writ in tuneful words of wood and stone,
And stood through reverent ages, a great Song
That sang in visible sacramental rhyme
Of Things Eternal in the years of Time.

II. As it Became.

And still through sound and silence flowed the stream,
But silence soon was rarer than the sound,
And men waxed dull of hearing, though it wound
Amongst them : and grew careless of the gleam
Which, night and day, from moon and sun, did seem
To bear Heav'n's light along this lower ground :
And few in all that sordid time were found
That looked or listened save to doubt or dream.
So that imperial poem that had graced
The generations with authentic power,
Letter and word, grew dimmed, disowned, defaced,
And only waited the all-ruining hour.
Yet still, as from and toward Eternity,
The River flowed from Sea-ward hill to Sea.

III. As it Is.

Then o'er the lands there moved a ghostly wind,
Breathed from the Mystic Sea and Holy Hill,
With healing on its wings: and, with a thrill,
As of the Spring, they woke; and, lo, the blind
Received their sight, and deaf men turned to find
There was such music in this world of ill
Of visible beauty, and gave heart and will
To glorify the Fane where it was shrined.
Then, one day of sweet Spring i' the Easter gleam,
More lovely, and with yet a lordlier strain,
That Poem, writ of old beside the Stream
Which maketh glad God's City, soared again—
Again, as from the Eternal Sea to Sea,
It sang the Oracle of the Things to be.

Hymns.

'I believe in the Holy Catholic Church, the Communion of Saints.'

'The Church of God, which He hath purchased with His own Blood.'
ACTS xx. 28.

THE Church's one Foundation
   Is JESUS CHRIST her Lord:
She is His new creation
   By water and the Word;
From heaven He came and sought her
   To be His holy Bride,
With His own Blood He bought her,
   And for her life He died.

Elect from every nation,
   Yet one o'er all the earth,
Her charter of salvation
   One LORD, one Faith, one Birth;
One Holy Name she blesses,
   Partakes one Holy Food,
And to one Hope she presses,
   With every grace endued.

The Church shall never perish!
    Her dear Lord to defend,
To guide, sustain, and cherish,
    Is with her to the end:
Though there be those who hate her,
    And false sons in her pale,
Against or foe or traitor
    She ever shall prevail.

Though with a scornful wonder
    Men see her sore opprest,
By schisms rent asunder,
    By heresies distrest;
Yet saints their watch are keeping,
    Their cry goes up, 'How long?'
And soon the night of weeping
    Shall be the morn of song.

Mid toil and tribulation,
    And tumult of her war,
She waits the consummation
    Of peace for evermore;
Till with the vision glorious
    Her longing eyes are blest,
And the great Church victorious
    Shall be the Church at rest.

Yet she on earth hath union
　　With FATHER, SPIRIT, SON,
And mystic sweet communion
　　With those whose rest is won:
With all her sons and daughters,
　　Who, by the Master's Hand
Led through the deathly waters,
　　Repose in Eden-land.

Oh, happy ones and holy!
　　LORD, give us grace that we
Like them, the meek and lowly,
　　On high may dwell with Thee!
There past the border mountains,
　　Where in sweet vales the Bride
With Thee by living fountains
　　For ever shall abide.
　　　　　　　　　Amen.

'*I believe in the Forgiveness of Sins.*'

'Her sins, which are many, are forgiven, for she loved much.'
ST. LUKE VII. 47.

WEARY of earth and laden with my sin,
    I look at heaven and long to enter in,
But there no evil thing may find a home—
And yet I hear a Voice that bids me 'Come.'

So vile I am, how dare I hope to stand
In the pure glory of that holy land?
Before the whiteness of that Throne appear?—
Yet there are Hands stretched out to draw me near.

The while I fain would tread the heavenly way,
Evil is ever with me day by day—
Yet on mine ears the gracious tidings fall,
'Repent, confess, thou shalt be loosed from all.'

It is the voice of JESUS that I hear,
His are the Hands stretched out to draw me near.

And His the Blood that can for all atone,
And set me faultless there before the Throne.

'Twas He Who found me on the deathly wild,
And made me heir of heaven, the FATHER's child,
And day by day, whereby my soul may live,
Gives me His grace of pardon, and will give.

O great Absolver, grant my soul may wear
The lowliest garb of penitence and prayer,
That in the FATHER's courts my glorious dress
May be the garment of Thy righteousness.

Yea, Thou wilt answer for me, Righteous LORD:
Thine all the merits, mine the great reward;
Thine the sharp thorns, so mine the golden crown,
Mine the life won, through Thine the life laid down.

Naught can I bring, dear LORD, for all I owe,
Yet let my full heart what it can bestow;
Like Mary's gift let my devotion prove,
Forgiven greatly, how I greatly love.
Amen.

Battle Hymn for the New Year.

'But let us, who are of the day, be sober, putting on the breastplate of faith and love; and for an helmet, the hope of salvation.'—1 THESS. v. 8.

THE old year's long campaign is o'er:
   Behold á new begun;
Not yet is closed the Holy War
   Not yet the triumph won:
Out of his still and deep repose
   We hear the old year say:—
'Go forth again to meet your foes,
   Ye children of the day!'

'Go forth! Firm Faith on every heart,
   Bright Hope on every helm,
Through that shall pierce no fiery dart,
   And this no fear o'erwhelm!
Go in the Spirit and the might
   Of Him Who led the way;
Close with the legions of the night,
   Ye children of the day!'

So forth we go to meet the strife,
  We will not fear nor fly!
Love we the holy warrior's life,
  His death we hope to die!
We slumber not, that charge in view,
  'Toil on while toil ye may,
Then night shall be no night to you,
  Ye children of the day!'

Lord God, our Glory, Three in One,
  Thine own sustain, defend!
And give, though dim this earthly sun,
  Thy true light to the end;
Till morning tread the darkness down,
  And night be swept away,
And infinite sweet triumph crown
  Thy children of the day!
                    Amen.

The River of God.

'There is a River, the streams whereof shall make glad the City of God.'—Psalm XLVI. 4.

    THERE is an ancient River,
        Whose streams descend in light
    From never-failing fountains
        Beyond all earthly sight;
    It ran through all the ages,
        And, wheresoe'er it flowed,
    Up rose the Holy City,
        The LORD's elect abode.

    The River still is flowing,
        But now with fuller stream:
    And still the light is falling,
        But now with brighter beam:

Of old the Song of Moses
  Soared as it swept along,
But now the name of JESUS
  Is made its sweeter Song.

Its radiance lights us onward,
  Its chanting waters cheer;
Blest is the eye beholding,
  Blest is the hearing ear;
For as the earth-clouds darken
  The glory clearer grows,
And gladder for life's tumult
  The stream of music flows.

GOD'S River! The One SPIRIT,
  Grace of the mystic SEVEN![1]
From Seaward mountain Seaward,
  From Heaven, it flows, to Heaven;
Fair City of these Waters!
  Cheered with their light and song,
So are thy children joyful,
  So are thy servants strong.

---

[1] Rev. i. 4.—'Grace be unto you . . . from the Seven Spirits which are before His Throne.' The Seven Spirits represent the Holy Spirit in His Sevenfold fulness.—*Wordsworth*.) So *S. Augustine:* ''The septenary number is consecrated to the Holy Ghost in Scripture'

O Beautiful, the River!
   The Church upon thy shore,
In bliss of expectation
   Abideth evermore,
Till at some holy even
   Her children on thy breast
From foretaste pass to fulness,
   From waiting into rest.
                    Amen.

Light at Eventide.

'At evening time it shall be light.'—ZECHARIAH XIV. 7.

NEED hath the Golden City none
 Of nightly moon or noon-day sun;
And every pilgrim waiting here
Till down from Heaven the Bride appear,
With this sure word may meet the night—
'At evening time it shall be light.'

With dull despairing gaze beyond,
The world would have my heart despond,
And cries, 'Life endeth with the tomb,
And after glory comes the gloom;'—
My soul, heed not the world's affright!
'At evening time it shall be light.'

The deep dark shades may whelm the day,
And all the splendours melt away,

The night may lower—but not for one
Whose life is hid beyond the sun;
My GOD shall make the darkness bright,
'At evening time it shall be light.'

It shall be light; and all below
My soul believed in, it shall know;
Unclouded then mine eyes shall see
The heart of every mystery:
In all Creation's depth and height
'At evening time it shall be light.'

It shall be light; when I behold
The Blessed Vision long foretold!
The dearest hope, the sweetest grace—
My soul's Beloved face to face.
Dear LORD, upon my longing sight
O bring the evening and the light!
Amen.

The Attraction of the Cross.

'I, if I be lifted up from the earth, will draw all men unto Me.'
ST. JOHN XII. 32.

IS there no hope for those who lie
   Among the dead about to die?
Writhing upon the great world's plain,
Martyrs of sin, in mortal pain;
The fiery taint upon them all
Of that Old Serpent of the Fall?

Yea, hearken! Israel, lift thine head,
O lie no longer with the dead!
For every care, for every crime,
There yet is hope, there yet is time:
Lift eye and heart: from yonder Tree
Release and Life look down on thee.

O look and listen! see thy LORD,
And hear His calm, absolving word;

O see, the balm of all thy woe,
Those precious drops of healing flow,
O hear, the word that sets thee free,
'Thou art redeemed—I die for thee.'

O see, the boundlessness of grace,
Those Arms of Love o'er-reaching space!
O hear, in final triumph hurled
His 'It is finished' o'er the world!
In that embrace, in that last breath,
Is seen, is said, the doom of death.

Death doomed, sin purged, the Serpent slain,
O dying soul, thou liv'st again!
Hold fast that life, and evermore
Look and believe, love and adore;
By all this gain and all that loss,
Lose never sight of yonder Cross!

Amen! for whither should I go?
Whom shall I find on earth below,
Whom shall I seek in Heav'n above,
For Hope and Healing, Life and Love,
Save Him Who hangs on yonder Tree?
Uplifted Lord! save only Thee?   Amen.

The Perfect Day.

'Until the Day break and the shadows flee away.'—CANTICLES II. 17.

DARK is the sky that overhangs my soul,
    The mists are thick that through the valley roll,
But as I tread I cheer my heart and say,
When the Day breaks the shadows flee away.

Unholy phantoms from the deep arise,
And gather through the gloom before mine eyes;
But all shall vanish at the dawning ray—
When the Day breaks the shadows flee away.

I bear the lamp my Master gave to me,
Burning and shining must it ever be,
And I must tend it till the night decay—
Till the Day break and shadows flee away.

He maketh all things good unto His own,
For them in every darkness light is sown;
He will make good the gloom of this my day—
Till that Day break and shadows flee away.

He will be near me in the awful hour
When the last Foe shall come in blackest power;
And He will hear me when at last I pray,
Let the Day break, the shadows flee away!

In Him, my God, my Glory, I will trust:
Awake and sing, O dweller in the dust!
Who shall come, will come, and will not delay—
His Day will break, those shadows flee away!
                                        Amen.

Holy Communion.

'Who loved me, and gave Himself for me.'—GALATIANS II. 20.

'REMEMBER Me: show forth My Death
    Until Mine Advent be:'
So of His Altar-Feast He saith
    Who gave Himself for me.

I will not tremble nor delay,
    Unworthy though I be:
He will not send my soul away
    Who gave Himself for me.

For there, when sorrows come to prove
    Where my true joy should be,
Most sweet the comfort of His Love
    Who gave Himself for me.

There, too, in calm of holy rest,
  My weary head shall be,
As if it lay upon His breast
  Who gave Himself for me.

There seem I ever nearest Home,
  Most sure of bliss to be
When in His glory He shall come
  Who gave Himself for me.

O that I ever may abide
  Where only life can be,
Still close and closer to His side
  Who gave Himself for me!
                    Amen.

The Travail of the Creation.

'The whole creation groaneth and travaileth in pain together until now.'—ROMANS VIII. 22.

THE whole creation groans and cries
    In travail of a second birth:
All living things, their covering skies,
    And circling floods, and parent earth,
Cry in an agonizing throng,
    How long, O LORD our GOD, how long?

How long? the living creatures cry,
    Subject to vanity with man;
Condemned to suffer and to die,
    Partakers of his righteous ban,
Yet doomed in hope that they may see
    And share the Church's liberty.

How long? the ruined skies complain,
    In prayer for the eternal calm;
With sighs of storm and tears of rain,
    They chant their lamentable psalm:

When shall the blissful light be born,
The beauty of Adoption's morn?

How long? the troubled waters moan:
  O visioned hope in hours of strife,
The jasper sea before the throne,
  Fed by the crystal stream of life!
O Israel's waters, stream and sea,
Fulness of peace and purity!

How long? all earth beneath the rod
  Of one wide curse lifts up her cry,
And waits, with all the sons of God,
  For their supreme Epiphany,
For their Redemption's glorious day,
When former things shall pass away.

How long, O LORD our GOD, how long?
  In this our earthly house of thrall,
With all creation's mighty throng,
  We too, Thine own, upon Thee call!
Patient in hope we long for home:—
Our Father, let Thy kingdom come.
                        Amen.

The Prisoners of Hope.

'Turn you to the Stronghold, ye prisoners of Hope.' ZECHARIAH IX. 2:.

YE faithful few of Israel's captive days,
    Who homeward ever fixed your faithful gaze,
Though far from home, your life was hidden there,
Prisoners of Hope, but victors of despair.

Ye of old time who waited for the LORD,
And turned you to the Stronghold of His Word,
Prisoners of Hope, ye could not be forlorn,
In depth of night so certain of the morn.

Ye of the good report in every age,
Who in that refuge met the tempest's rage,
Prisoners of Hope, ye knew the strife would cease,
And in its wildest hour foretasted peace.

O turn ye thither, ye who lie so low,
With sin beset or desolate in woe;
Up, from the dust where ye so long have lain!
The Rock of Ages was not cleft in vain!

Prisoners of Hope, there shall ye rest awhile,
Watching in peace the starry promise smile,
Willing to keep your vigil till at last
Hope's gentle tyranny be overpast.

O word of Christ, that cannot pass away,
The Church's Stronghold in her evil day,
Turn we to thee, whatever foe prevail,
On the wild hill, or in the solemn vale!

To thee we turn, until our souls shall hear
The King we serve, the LORD we love, draw near:
And we shall change, when His command is given,
Hope's happy prison-house for happier Heaven.
         Amen.

The Glorious Three.

*'Now abideth Faith, Hope, Charity, these three; but the greatest of these is Charity.'—*1 Corinthians XIII. 13.

FAITH, who sees beyond the portal
    Of far Heaven with eagle eyes;
Hope foretasting life immortal;
    Charity, in meekest guise—
Now abide the glorious three,
    But the first is Charity.

Faith abideth, there are mountains
    She must day by day remove;
By the fair refreshing fountains
    Hope abideth; and sweet Love
Standeth crowned, the twain between,
Very lowly, yet the queen.

So, in view of things eternal,
    Rocks of time are over-hurl'd;
So, behold, a beauty vernal
    Robes the winter of the world;

But where Charity hath trod
Is the path of Very GOD.

Those shall vanish: she remaineth
   When their work and life are o'er:
As below, above, she reigneth,
   So she shall reign evermore;
Heaven and earth shall pass away—
Love goes ruling on for aye.

Faith and Preaching find an ending,
   Hope and Prayer together cease;
Love and Praise, together blending,
   Know no changing save increase;
When that cry is past—'How long?'
Love takes up an endless song.

Now the old world is a-dying,
   'Soon,' cries Faith, 'will Christ appear;
Hope with rapture is replying,
   'Then the reign of Love is near;'
Willing both to fade away,
Star-like, at her perfect day.
                  Amen.

The 'Athletes of the Universe.'[1]

'Destitute, afflicted, tormented : of whom the world was not worthy.'
HEBREWS xi. 37, 38.

THEIR names are names of kings
    Of heavenly line,
The bliss of earthly things
    Who did resign.

Chieftains they were, who warr'd
    With sword and shield ;
Victors for GOD the LORD
    On foughten field.

Sad were their days on earth,
    Mid hate and scorn ;
A life of pleasure's dearth,
    A death forlorn.

[1] An expression used by S. Chrysostom.

Yet blest that end in woe,
   And those sad days;
Only man's blame below—
   Above, GOD's praise!

A city of great name
   Was built for them,
Of glorious golden fame—
   Jerusalem.

Redeemed with precious Blood
   From death and sin,
Sons of the Triune GOD,
   They entered in.

So did the life of pain
   In glory close;
LORD GOD, may we attain
   Their grand repose!
                Amen.

The Church's Song.

'My Beloved is mine, and I am His.'—CANTICLES II. 16.

I AM Thine: I stand before Thee,
   JESU, evermore Thine own:
Not by merit, but by glory
  Of Thy grace, elect alone,
    Thy beloved,
  Unto men and angels shown.

Thou art mine: I did not choose Thee,
  Only came when Thou didst call;
Now, oh never let me lose Thee,
  From Thy favour never fall!
    My Beloved,
  First and last, and all in all.

I am Thine: Thy word remaineth,
  That no creature far or nigh,

Where the lord of evil reigneth
  In deep hell or haunted sky,
    Shall for ever
  Part of love the mystic tie.

Thou art mine :—although Thy Vision
  Fills not yet my longing sight,
Though the doubting world's derision
  Holds my honour in despite,—
    Mine in darkness,
  Surely as at last in light!

I am Thine : in tribulation
  From Thy parted Heavens above
Comes divinest consolation,
  Lighting as the Holy Dove
    With the message
  Of thine everlasting love.

Thou art mine : in bliss and sorrow,
  In the shade as in the shine :
Yesterday, to-day, to-morrow,
  To the age of ages,—mine ;
    Yea, my Master,
  Mine Thou art, for I am Thine.

        Amen.

Hymn of Thanksgiving for the Recovery of H.R.H. The Prince of Wales.

SUNG IN ST. PAUL'S CATHEDRAL[1] ON FEB. 27, 1872.

'Turn our captivity, O Lord, as the streams in the south. They that sow in tears shall reap in joy. He that goeth forth and weepeth, bearing precious seed, shall doubtless come again with rejoicing, bringing his sheaves with him.'—Ps. CXXVI. 4-6.

LORD of our souls' salvation!
    LORD of our earthly weal!
We who in tribulation
    Did for Thy mercy kneel,
Lift up glad hearts before Thee,
    And eyes no longer dim,
And for Thy grace adore Thee
    In eucharistic hymn.

[1] The Hymn is here given in full form as it was generally sung throughout the country; but, owing to the necessary restriction as to time in the Cathedral service, a selection of four verses only—the 1st, a combination of the 2d and 4th, the 6th, and the 7th,—was adapted by the Author for use in St. Paul's.

When vine and fig-tree languish,
    And every fount is dry,
When hearts in supreme anguish
    To Thee lift up their cry:
Then doth Thy love deliver!
    From Thine unshortened hand
Joy, like the southern river,
    O'erflows the weary land.

Lay dark o'er field and city
    Death's shadow, and in fear
To thee, O LORD of Pity,
    GOD of the hearing ear!
By the dear Grace that bought us
    We cried as in the night,
And lo! the morning brought us
    From Thee the living light.

Went forth the nation weeping,
    With precious seed of prayer,
Hope's awful vigil keeping
    'Mid rumours of despair,

Now, to Thy glory bringing
   Its sheaves of praise along,
Again it cometh singing
   A happy harvest song.

O sweet and divine fashion
   Of Grace sublime in power!
That meteth out compassion
   By sorrow's direst hour:
O Love, most high, most holy!
   The merciful in might,
That unto hearts most lowly
   Is ever Depth and Height.

Bless Thou our adoration!
   Our gladness sanctify!
Be this rejoicing nation
   To Thee by joy more nigh:
Oh be this great Thanksgiving,
   That with one voice we raise,
Wrought into holier living
   Through all our after days.

Bless, FATHER, him Thou gavest
   Back to the loyal land;
O SAVIOUR, him Thou savest
   Still cover with Thine Hand;
O SPIRIT, the Defender,
   Be his to guard and guide,
Now in life's mid-day splendour,
   On to the eventide!
                     Amen.

The Transfiguration.

'And when the Voice was past, Jesus was found alone.'
ST. LUKE IX. 36.

DEEPLY dark and deeply still
    Midnight wraps the lonely hill,
And the Three are keeping there,
By the Master in His prayer,
Drooping watch to slumber prone,
Till the Master prays alone.

Lo! in sudden awe they rise:
Sudden splendour fills their eyes:
Sorrow-marred the Master's Face
Lightens with unearthly grace,
Excellence of glory [1] now
Robes His form from foot to brow!

[1] See 2 St. Peter i. 17.

And beside Him there are seen
Other Two in heavenly sheen;
Prophecy and Law are there:
Quick and Dead[1] the glory share:
Twain, who found the morning light
At the noon and through the night.

These in solemn sweet accord
Hold high converse with the Lord:
Till is heard the Voice profound
Through the lightning shade[2] around:
Till it passes—and anon
Gaze they on The Christ alone.

So the Church, in vigil still
On the dark world's lonely hill,
Slumber-laden hardly heeds
While the God-man intercedes,
Till upon her eyes He shine
With a glory all-divine.

---

[1] Moses who had died; Elias who had never seen death. So Christ was shown to be 'Lord both of the dead and of the living.'—See S. Chrysostom.

[2] 'A bright cloud overshadowed them.' If we may so say, Light is God's shade. He 'dwells in a privacy of glorious light.' See Wordsworth, St. Matt. xvii. 5.

So the sacred types of old
Their last witness shall unfold ;
So like stars before the day
In His light shall pass away ;
So the quick and dead shall own
Christ is Lord and Christ alone.

FATHER, by that oracle
From the gleaming cloud that fell,
SPIRIT, by th' attesting word
From the Law and Prophets heard,
Grant that all Thy Church be one
In the Glory of the SON.
Amen.

Hymns for the Day of Intercession.

I.—FOR COLONIAL MISSIONS.

'Now are they many members, yet but one body.'—1 COR. XII. 20.

FAR off our brethren's voices
   Are borne from alien lands,
Far off our Father's children
   Reach out their waiting hands.
'Give us,' they cry, 'our portion;
   Co-heirs of grace divine!
Give us the Word of promise,
   Give us the Three-fold line.'

Yea, though the world of waters
   Between us ever rolls,
No ocean wastes may sever
   The brotherhood of souls;

Far from us, they are of us;
   No bound of all the earth
May part the sons and daughters
   Who share the second birth.

In happiest homely commune,
   When sweetest songs are sung
Awakes those alien echoes
   One sacred mother-tongue.
Then let us praise together!
   Together let us pray,
And go together Homeward
   Upon the ancient way.

Together Heavenward, Homeward;
   For ever in our view
One spiritual City—
   Jerusalem the New;
For ever drawing nearer
   To ONE belov'd, adored,
The Crucified Who bought us,
   The Crown'd Incarnate Lord.

Lord God! Eternal Father!
    Send down the Holy Dove,
For His dear sake Who loved us,
    To quicken us in love.
Bless us with His compassion,
    That we, or ere we rest,
May work to bless our brethren,
    And, blessing, be more blest!

And lo, we pray, rejoicing!
    We praise Thee in our prayer!
Lo, o'er the wide world mingles
    Our incense on the air:
So pleading we adore Thee,
    God of the hearing ear!
Thou Who so late hast heard us
    Vouchsafe again to hear!
                  Amen.

The Same.

II.—FOR MISSIONS TO THE HEATHEN.

'Come over into Macedonia and help us!'—ACTS XVI. 9.

THROUGH midnight gloom from Macedon
    The cry of myriads as of one,
The voiceful silence of despair,
Is eloquent in awful prayer;
The soul's exceeding bitter cry,
'Come o'er and help us or we die.'

How mournfully it echoes on,
For half the world is Macedon!
These brethren to their brethren call,
And by the Love which loved them all,

And by the whole world's Life they cry,
'O ye that live, behold we die!'

By other sounds our ears are won
Than that which wails from Macedon;
The roar of gain is round us rolled,
Or we unto ourselves are sold,
And cannot list the alien cry
'O hear and help us lest we die!'

Yet with that cry from Macedon
The very car of Christ rolls on!
'I come: who would abide My day,
In yonder wilds prepare My way!
My voice is crying in their cry
Help ye the dying lest ye die!'

O once, for men, of man the Son,
Yea, Thine the cry from Macedon!
O by the Kingdom and the Power
And Glory of Thine advent hour,
Wake heart and will to hear their cry,
Help us to help them lest we die!

Yet fair the hope that speeds us on
With psalms of praise for Macedon!
Thy blessing given, Thy promise bright,
Are earnest sweet of morning light,
Till 'Alleluia' be the cry
Of souls that live and shall not die!

         Amen.

The Same.

III.—HYMN OF THANKSGIVING.

'Blessed be the Lord God, the God of Israel, Who only doeth wondrous things; and blessed be His glorious name for ever: and let the whole earth be filled with His glory. Amen and Amen.'—Ps. LXXII. 18-19.

LORD of the harvest! it is right and meet
 That we should lay our first fruits at Thy feet
   With joyful Alleluia.

Sweet is the soul's thanksgiving after prayer;
Sweet is the worship that with Heaven we share
   Who sing the Alleluia!

Lowly we prayed, and Thou didst hear on high—
Didst lift our hearts and change our suppliant cry
   To festal Alleluia.

So sing we now in tune with that great song
That all the age of ages shall prolong,
    The endless Alleluia.

To Thee, O LORD of Harvest, Who hast heard,
And to Thy white-robed reapers given the word,
    We sing our Alleluia.

O CHRIST, Who in the wide world's ghostly sea
Hast bid the net be cast anew, to Thee
    We sing our Alleluia.

To Thee, Eternal SPIRIT, Who again
Hast moved with life upon the slumbrous main,
    We sing our Alleluia.

Yea, West and East the companies go forth:
'We come!' is sounding to the South and North;
    To GOD sing Alleluia!

The fishermen of JESUS far away
Seek in new waters an immortal prey;
    To CHRIST sing Alleluia!

The Holy DOVE is brooding o'er the deep,
And careless hearts are waking out of sleep;
    To HIM sing Alleluia!

Yea, for sweet hope new-born—blest work begun—
Sing Alleluia to the THREE IN ONE,
   Adoring Alleluia !

Glory to GOD ! the Church in patience cries ;
Glory to GOD ! the Church at rest replies,
   With endless Alleluia !
      Amen.

Saint Mark,

EVANGELIST AND MARTYR.

'Mark departed from them from Pamphylia, and went not with them to the work.'—ACTS xv. 38.
'Take Mark . . . profitable to me for the ministry.'—2 TIM. IV. 11.

BY Paul at war in Gentile lands
    The Son of Consolation[1] stands;
Together, in the evil day,
They set Christ's battle in array:
Yet mourn for one, in darker hour,
By fear o'erthrown from faith and power.

Rejoice not,[2] O thou ghostly foe,
Albeit thy wiles have laid him low!

---
[1] Barnabas, the Son of Consolation, a Levite.—Acts iv. 36.
[2] Micah vii. 8.

For, rising from the battle-plain,
Cast down, but not destroyed, again
He shall fulfil, with lowlier heart,
The contrite Christian's braver part.

The voice that, in his bitter need,
Did for the father[1] intercede,
Shall for the fallen son prevail:
In meeker faith he shall not fail!
But with remorseful memory rife
Shall wage a surer, sterner strife.

Now tremble! for, behold, he stands
And lifts in power the hanging hands,
The feeble knees are braced and strong,
And—hushed awhile—his battle-song
Is breathed once more in holy shame,
Thy challenge in the awful Name.

Lo, spoils for Christ in Babylon![2]
For Christ the Morian's land[3] is won!

---

[1] Early Church history attributes to St. Mark an intimate connexion with St. Peter, asserting that he wrote his Gospel under St. Peter's eye. Cf. 1 St. Peter v. 13, 'Marcus, my son.'

[2] See 1 St. Peter v. 13.

[3] We have St. Jerome's authority for asserting, that St. Mark was appointed by St. Peter first Bishop of Alexandria, in Egypt.

Till now, the long campaign complete,
He offers at his Captain's feet—
So gained by loss—with latest breath
The life he loved not to the death.

LORD GOD, THE FATHER, grant us here
The fearless courage of Thy fear;
LORD GOD, THE CHRIST, so in our need,
When faith is failing, intercede;
LORD GOD, THE SPIRIT, thus amend,
And keep us constant to the end.
Amen.

Battle Hymn of Church Defence.

DEDICATED TO THE 'CHURCH SOCIETY' OF ST. PAUL'S, HAGGERSTON.

"Her foundations are upon the holy hills: the Lord loveth the gates of Zion more than all the dwellings of Jacob."—Ps. LXXXVII. 1, 2.
"God is in the midst of her, therefore shall she not be removed: God shall help her, and that right early."—Ps. XLVI. 5.
"If I forget thee, O Jerusalem, let my right hand forget her cunning."—Ps. CXXXVII. 5.

ROUND the Sacred City gather
    Egypt, Edom, Babylon;
All the warring hosts of error,
    Sworn against her, are as one:
Vain the leaguer! her foundations
    Are upon the holy hills,
And the love of the ETERNAL
    All her stately temple fills.

Get thee, watchman, to the rampart!
    Gird thee, warrior, with thy sword!
And be strong as ye remember
    In your midst is GOD the LORD:

Like the night-mists from the valley,
   These shall vanish, one by one,
Egypt's malice, Edom's envy,
   And the hate of Babylon.

But be true, ye sons and daughters,
   Lest the peril be within;
Watch to prayer, lest in your slumber
   Stealthy foemen enter in;
Safe the mother and the children
   If their will and love be strong,
While their loyal hearts go singing
   Prayer and praise for battle-song.

Church of GOD! if we forget thee,
   Let His blessing fail our hand;
When our love shall not prefer thee,
   Let His love forget our land—
Nay! our memory shall be steadfast
   Though in storm the mountains shake,
And our love is love for ever,
   For it is for JESUS' sake.

Church of JESUS! His thy Banner
   And thy Banner's awful Sign:

By His passion and His glory
   Thou art His and He is thine:
From the Hill of His Redemption
   Flows thy sacramental tide:
From the Hill of His Ascension
   Flows the grace of God thy Guide.

Yea: thou Church of GOD the SPIRIT!
   His Society Divine,
His the living Word thou keepest,
   His thy Apostolic line,
Ancient prayer and song liturgic,
   Creeds that change not to the end,
As His gift we have received them,
   As His charge we will defend.

Alleluia, Alleluia,
   To the FATHER, SPIRIT, SON,
In Whose will the Church at warfare
   With the Church at rest is one:
So to THEE we sing in union,
   GOD in earth and Heav'n adored,
Alleluia, Alleluia,
   Holy, Holy, Holy LORD.
                      Amen.

Confirmation Litany Hymn.[1]

"Greater is He that is in you, than he that is in the world."
1 St. John iv. 4

O THOU, by Whom the saints abide,
    Whatever fears or foes betide,
Safe in the Bridegroom and the Bride:
        God the Spirit, hear us.

O Thou, Who art the Gift unpriced
That for the poorest hath sufficed,
With grace and peace from Jesus Christ;
        God the Spirit, hear us.

O Thou, Who for the awful fight
With more than mortal will and might
Hast ever armed the sons of light:
        God the Spirit, hear us.

[1] May be used also at Adult Baptisms.

Arm those who kneel before Thee now—
Let the dear Sign upon their brow
In every heart seal every vow:
        God the Spirit, hear us.

Dread is the war they now begin,
But stronger Thou their souls within
Than all the power of Adam's sin!
        God the Spirit, hear us.

O by their death in Him Who died!
Their life in Him, the Glorified!
Keep them for ever at His side:
        God the Spirit, hear us.

So may they through the hosts of ill
Go on from strength to strength, until
They win the peaceful Holy Hill:
        God the Spirit, hear us.

So, by Thy grace in Him to-day,
In Him be every soul for aye
When Heaven and Earth have passed away:
        God the Spirit, hear us.

Through vigils late and labours long,
Through all world-weariness and wrong,
So guide them to Thine evensong:
  God the Spirit, hear us.

The song of work in weakness done,
The song of rest by mercy won,
The song of endless life begun:
  God the Spirit, hear us.
        Amen.

'In Thee.'

A HYMN FOR CHURCH-WORKERS.

DEDICATED TO THE 'CHURCH SOCIETY' OF ST. PAUL'S, HAGGERSTON.

'Christ the Power of God, and the Wisdom of God. . . . Of Him are ye in Christ Jesus.'— 1 COR. I. 24 and 30.

CHRIST, the Wisdom and the Power!
From our labour's fleeting hour
To that timeless age of bliss
Which shall crown the toil of this,
Grant that all our life may be
Hidden and revealed 'in Thee.'

That our work may be divine
Seek we not our own but Thine ;
Lost to self and found 'in Thee,'
Find we sweet Humility,

Zeal by reverent Love refined,
True Devotion's single mind.

So 'in Thee' we shall be strong,
Seem the labour light or long;
And, though clouds of self and sin
Darken round us and within,
So not dimly shall we see
Light to lighten all 'in Thee.'

Thus, 'in Thee,' O Wisdom, wise,
May we touch the blinded eyes,
Turn the steps that vainly roam
Back to happiness and home,
And in sacred waters sweet
Wash Thy young disciples' feet.

Thus 'in Thee,' O Power, we go
Through Thy Church's war below,
In Thy panoply alway
Steadfast through the evil day;
Troubled ever, not distrest,
Moving to Thy Church at rest.

'In Thee' now, and 'in Thee' then!
Now, and when Thou com'st again;
Now at war among Thy foes,
Then at peace in Thy repose,
Brother-man and Sovran-Lord
Thine our Work and our Reward!

Amen.

www.ingramcontent.com/pod-product-compliance
Lightning Source LLC
Chambersburg PA
CBHW032046220426
43664CB00008B/888